THEOLOGY:
Reclaiming the Relevance

Daniel Mann

THEOLOGY

Copyright 2016 by Daniel Mann

Printed in the United States of America

The Bible versions used in this publication are:

Mann, Daniel, author
Misheff, Van, editor

THEOLOGY:
Reclaiming the Relevance

And he said to him,
"You shall love the Lord your God with all your heart
and with all your soul and with all your mind.
This is the great and first commandment."
Matthew 22:37-38

THEOLOGY: Reclaiming the Relevance

Part I

THEOLOGY: NO LONGER RELEVANT?

continued...

THEOLOGY:
Reclaiming the Relevance

Part II

THEOLOGY:
GOD'S PLAN AND REQUIREMENT

INTRODUCTION

My students complain often about the various introduction-to-theology textbooks that they have been assigned. They tell me that all those books tend to be abstract, with precious few Scripture verses to illustrate the principles. They complain about unfamiliar terminology, especially words and concepts they have never seen in the pages of Scripture.

This book seeks to correct those issues.

I am not trying to say that there is not a place for those kinds of texts. They serve to connect their readers to the theological discussions and controversies of the past, appropriately using the terminology of the past. This perspective, of course, is necessary.

However, before we ask serious Christians and students of the Word to grapple with the weighty issues of those who came before us, there is a crucial need for a book that will first of all make valid connections with the theological challenges that are confronting us today, using terminology and language with which we are all familiar.

I want all those who study the Bible to understand that theology can speak to them exactly where they are in life, right now. A good understanding of theology can help us to face our confusion and dispel our fears. Solid theological thinking is essential in every area of our lives. I want people to see the truths of the Bible as the precious jewels that they are.

This kind of foundational theology is more needful today than perhaps ever before. We are increasingly being confronted with negative messages about the Bible and theology, even within the Church. On an increasingly regular basis, we Christians are being told that:

> *…faith is only about believing, and not trying to figure things out;*
> *…feeling and experiencing are more important than thinking;*
> *…a relationship with Christ is about closing the mind so that we might experience Him directly;*
> *…doctrine divides;*
> *…clinging to fundamentalist beliefs divides us from others and even from God;*
> *…theology is sterile and lifeless;*
> *…theology and our distinctive doctrines and beliefs cause wars;*
> *…theological certainty is not a possibility.*

The mind-set represented in this list of untruths is doing great damage to the theology that can set men and women free. Moreover, the general acceptance of this kind of thinking has made theology into a dirty word. As a consequence, serious attempts to understand the Bible are becoming increasingly rare.

It is my prayer that this will change and that this volume might make a small contribution towards *reclaiming the relevance of theology!*

Chapter 1

CHRISTIAN LIFE: WHAT IS OUR FOUNDATION?

CHAPTER SUMMARY
The entire Christian life is founded upon what we know and believe—theology. Our welfare depends largely on receiving the wisdom that comes from God. Therefore, our thinking is a center of spiritual warfare. That is why the Bible warns us so often about false beliefs.

Theology is no longer relevant, according to some who call themselves Christians.

Here is how a friend counselled me:

> *The Bible is good for starters, but there comes a time to get off the training wheels. God respects us enough to allow us to pursue some independence!*

According to my friend, there comes a time when believers need to leave behind the dos-and-don'ts of the Bible and begin to concentrate their efforts on love, experience, and social justice. But is this actually an either/or issue? Should we ever "graduate" and move on from the Word of God and the foundational theology it teaches?

Not according to any of the teachings of the Bible.

Jesus quoted a verse that was fifteen hundred years old to demonstrate the fact that the words of Scripture never lose their relevance in any time period of history, including our own:

- Jesus answered [the devil], "It is written: 'Man does not live on bread alone, but on *every word that comes from the mouth of God*'" (Matthew 4:4, emphasis added).

We need to keep in mind here that Jesus was actually quoting Deuteronomy 8:3. Not only were these ancient words still relevant in New Testament times, they were the words that Jesus Himself had relied upon in the midst of His own temptation in the wilderness.

Evidently, our Lord chose not to let go of His "training wheels." Why then should we?

Likewise, should we pick and choose verses in the Bible to ascertain which words are still relevant for our day? Or should we—like Jesus—embrace "every word" of Scripture?

When He sent out His disciples for the last time during His earthly ministry, Jesus instructed them…

- "…teaching them to obey *everything I have commanded you*. And surely I am with you always, to the very end of the age" (Matthew 28:20, emphasis added).

There is no indication anywhere in Scripture that these teachings were meant to be used merely to get us started in our lives of faith and then, later on, were to be abandoned.

Those who disagree with our position go so far as to claim that "Bible-believing Christians" actually worship the Bible. Instead of idolatry, they charge us with "bibliolatry," an idolatrous form of worship that elevates the Bible over the worship of the one true God.

However, when we study what Jesus said, we find that He exalted the Word of God above everything else:

- "Heaven and earth will pass away, but my words will never pass away" (Matthew 24:35).

In fact, other parts of the Bible place God's Words on an equal footing with God Himself:

- I will bow down toward your holy temple and will praise your name for your love and your faithfulness, for you have exalted above all things your name [God Himself] *and your word* (Psalm 138:2, emphasis added).

To worship God was and is to worship Him according to His revelation. In fact, He insists that our love for Him is measured by our obedience to His Word:

- "Whoever has my commands and obeys them, he is the one who loves me. He who loves me will be loved by my Father, and I too will love him and show myself to him" (John 14:21).

God and His Word are inseparable. Consequently, when we despise and disobey His Word, it is the same as despising *Him*:

- "Why did you *despise the word of the LORD* by doing what is evil in his eyes? You struck down Uriah the Hittite with the sword and took his wife to be your own. You killed him with the sword of the Ammonites. Now, therefore, the sword will never depart from your house, *because you despised me* [God] and took the wife of Uriah the Hittite to be your own" (2 Samuel 12:9-10, emphasis added).

This is serious business.

When we despise the Lord's Word, we not only despise the Lord, we are actually *blaspheming* Him, as well:

- "'But anyone who sins defiantly…blasphemes the LORD, and that person must be cut off from his people. Because he has despised the LORD'S word and broken his commands, that person must surely be cut off; his guilt remains on him'" (Numbers 15:30-31).

The way we respond to Scripture is the way we respond to the Lord. Therefore, we cannot say that we love the Lord if we reject His Word. In fact, one of the requirements for having a relationship with the Lord is that we abide in His Word, His teaching:

- Anyone who runs ahead and does not continue in the teaching of Christ does not have God; whoever continues in the teaching has both the Father and the Son (2 John 9).

Let's not take the training wheels off our bikes anytime soon.

*   *   *   *   *

It is clear that Scripture is to inform *every area of our lives*— even the way we worship and pray.

Jesus clearly was not a religious pluralist, one who believed that all religions are okay. He had warned a Samaritan woman that her religion was not adequate. It was not of the truth, in contrast to the religion given to the Jews:

- "You Samaritans worship what you do not know; we worship what we do know, for salvation is from the [revelation given to the] Jews. Yet a time is coming and has now come when the true worshipers will worship the Father in spirit and truth, for they are the kind of worshipers the Father seeks. God is spirit, and his worshipers must worship in spirit and in truth" (John 4:22-24).

According to Jesus, God's truth was the necessary ingredient, the very thing that the Samaritans lacked. Those who worship God "must worship in spirit and in truth." Worshiping according to the truth was not an option. Even if the woman at the well had been sincere about her religion—sincerity being regarded as one of the highest virtues by many—this mind-set would still not have been adequate for her salvation.

The Bible—God's Word—provides us with the strongest of foundations for our faith. We never graduate from the truth of the Scriptures. Instead, we are counselled to meditate on His Word day and night for our own well-being (Joshua 1:8).

Let us find our delight in the law of the LORD:

> But his delight is in the law of the LORD,
> and on his law he meditates day and night.
> He is like a tree planted by streams of water,
> which yields its fruit in season
> and whose leaf does not wither.
> Whatever he does prospers.
> Psalm 1:2-3

Chapter 2

IDEOLOGY AND THEOLOGY: WHAT IS THE POSTMODERN PERSPECTIVE?

CHAPTER SUMMARY
The Emergent Church's Tony Jones and Eckhart Tolle are both gurus of religions without a theology. However— illogically—they have many theological things to say about their religions and against the Christian religion.

In today's postmodern world, theology and even truth have become dirty words. Instead, smorgasbord religion reigns:

> *Whatever feels right is right! Choose what seems right for you and discard anything distasteful. You need not fill your plate with anything that makes you feel the slightest bit of guilt or shame. And truth? Well, truth isn't on the table either, since "truth" is just a matter of your own inclinations and choice.*

With a religion like this, you would no longer be able to make any objective judgments about anything. But, the "up" side of all this is that no one would be able to judge you either.

Oprah Winfrey's onetime guru, Eckhart Tolle, is a good example of those who espouse this kind of thinking:

- "If you go deep enough in your religion, then you all get to the same place. It's a question of going deeper, so there's no conflict here. The important thing is that religion doesn't become an ideology...the moment you say 'only my belief' or 'our belief' is true, and you deny other people's beliefs, then you've adopted an ideology. And then religion becomes a closed door" (Nozaki 12-19).

For Tolle, it's all about what you experience, not what you believe or think. There can be no correct theology or ideology because, according to Tolle, any written-down, established collection of thoughts would slam the door on "other people's beliefs."

However, everything that Tolle has written demonstrates that he has his own ideology—which he believes is true—as opposed to other ideologies. We must remember that having a theology or ideology is unavoidable. Once you have articulated what you have experienced and defined what it means, you are promoting an ideology.

Clearly, Eckhart Tolle is presenting one of the many appealingly-packaged forms of New Age theology. In doing this, he is violating the very rule that he has declared inviolable—to *not* adopt an ideology. Besides this, he is telling everyone else that they are wrong to think that they are ideologically right. But isn't Tolle asserting that *he* is ideologically right in his judgment of *their* ideology?

I understand totally how New Age theology has become attractive to so many people. It places us in the driver's seat as the final arbiter of "truth," in whatever form that truth might take. As a consequence, we are still stuck with a belief system, whether we want one or not.

So then, if this is the case, it is important that we have an accurate belief system. After all, our beliefs about reality serve as a roadmap that enables us to navigate life's pathways with the least frustration and the fewest cliff-hangers.

Our beliefs also serve as our eyes. They determine what we see and how we respond to what we see. If we see all others as our friends, we will respond with open arms. If we see them as enemies, we will keep our distance.

Instead of seeing the world through either of these distorted perspectives, we need a set of lenses that enables us to see others as they really are.

We also need to see ourselves accurately. Managing our lives well depends on our having a set of lenses that brings both who we are individually and our external world into a fine-tuned focus.

The Bible provides that lens.

I was a slave to the hopeless preoccupation of evaluating myself according to my performance and what others thought of me. Each failure and rejection became a threat to my well-being. However, God's Word eventually freed me from this obsession. Through the study of the Scriptures, I came to understand that it's not about me and my success. Rather, it's all about what Christ accomplished:

- If God is for us, who can be against us? He who did not spare his own Son, but gave him up for us all—how will he not also, along with him, graciously give us all things? (Romans 8:31-32)

The more I grew in this confidence, the less other people's opinions mattered.

Our beliefs will either free us or imprison us. In fact, I agree wholeheartedly with Tolle that religion can be a "closed door." My faith in Christ has closed the door to depression, painful obsessions, and many other psycho-parasites. If these are the sorts of things that are left out in the cold, then I have no problem with this type of closed-door policy, none at all.

At the same time, however, theology can also represent a door that is wide open, serving to draw people in.

If our theology represents an accurate roadmap of reality, it provides an objective common ground, a place where people can meet and share the same language. And, if our theology is one of love, it can reach beyond our divisions to embrace those on the other side.

Fear and disdain can be great obstacles. However, if our theology instructs us to trust in a God who is all-powerful and all-protecting, we are encouraged and empowered to stretch ourselves beyond our comfort zone, as our Lord commands us:

- "But seek first the kingdom of God and his righteousness, and all these things will be added to you. Therefore do not be anxious about tomorrow, for tomorrow will be anxious for itself. Sufficient for the day is its own trouble" (Matthew 6:33-34).

* * * * *

In addition to what New-Agers have said, the Emergent Church (EC) brings a similar indictment against theology. EC guru Tony Jones has written:

- "This fixation with [theological] propositions can easily lead to the attempt to use the finite tool of language on an absolute Presence that transcends and embraces finite reality. Languages are culturally constructed symbol systems that enable humans to communicate by designating one finite reality in distinction from another. The truly infinite God of Christian faith is beyond all our linguistic [theological] grasping…and so *the struggle to capture God in our finite propositional structures is nothing short of linguistic idolatry"* (Jones 234, emphasis added).

If we are unable to capture anything of God through our doctrinal "structures," and if all of our attempts represent "idolatry," then shouldn't these same charges of idolatry come back to indict Jones? For is he not as well attempting to disseminate certain timeless spiritual truths in the books he writes?

Of course, that is exactly what he is doing!

As far as the Christian faith is concerned, our Lord actually instructs us "…to capture God in our finite propositional structures." In fact, these doctrinal structures help us to understand how a relationship with God is indeed possible. He leads us into knowledge about Who He is in order that we might enter into a personal relationship with Him:

- We know also that the Son of God has come and has given us understanding, so that we may know him who is true. And we are in him who is true—even in his Son Jesus Christ. He is the true God and eternal life (1 John 5:20).

Jesus also prayed about our knowledge of God and the way that it prepares us for a life-changing relationship with Him:

- "I have made you known [doctrinally] to them, and will continue to make you known in order that the love you have for me may be in them and that I myself may be in them" (John 17:26).

Doctrine—the knowledge of God—is essential for our entire life.

One Christian I know gave me a poignant example that makes this point well. She had been tormented by the fact that she was not experiencing the joy that she thought was to be hers as a Christian. However, she learned from Scripture that the hardships in her life were necessary in order to make her more like her Savior (2 Corinthians 4:10-11; Hebrews 12:5-11). Now she *knows* that there is indeed a purpose for all her trials. As a result of learning this biblical truth, she is now eager to patiently endure whatever God allows to come into her life. Doctrine has enabled her to find, not only cognitive rest, but true peace, as well.

This reminds me of my own experience. While working for the NYC Department of Probation, I had experienced a great deal of rejection from my co-workers. Already having a strong tendency to feel rejected, I found this extra burden devastating. These experiences seemed to indict me as an inadequate failure of a person. However, these same challenges also drove me deeper into Scripture, which led me to a renewed understanding of my Savior's unfathomable love for me (Ephesians 3:16-20).

My painful feelings also deepened my resolve to define myself only according to what was important to God, not what others might say or do:

- Fear of man will prove to be a snare, but whoever trusts in the Lord is kept safe (Proverbs 29:25).

Over-concern about the opinions of others will kill us. However, when our ultimate concern is invested in *God's opinions*, we find life. I can now look back on those painful days with thanksgiving. He taught me so much through them. And of course, Scripture played an essential role in that spiritual victory.

In contrast to the blessings that come from studying the Word of God and the sound doctrine associated with it, Tony Jones writes:

- "Giving in to the pressure to petrify the conversation in a 'statement' would make [the] Emergent [Church] easier to control; its critics could dissect it and then place it in a theological museum alongside other dead conceptual specimens…" (Jones 235)

Coming to a firm doctrinal resting place is something that Jones associates with calcification, death, and even the formaldehyde that preserves specimens.

Since, according to Jones, "truth" is in constant flux, those who follow his line of thinking have no mental resting place—nothing to lean on in the midst of doubts and fears. Admittedly, Emergent Church adherents are encouraged to search for answers, ask questions, and discuss. But there can never be any actual finding of answers or resolution of difficulties.

And why not?

Simply this: once any answers are found, those truths would then become like a museum's "dead conceptual specimens," useful only for further dissection and manipulation.

Jones is searching for answers without any expectation of actually finding them. Although he himself writes so that he can persuade others, once these others are persuaded—according to his own theory—they too will become like "dead…specimens," ready to be stored on a dusty shelf.

Both Jones and Tolle are products of our postmodern age. It is an age that denies both the importance and even the existence of truth, even as both men promote their own brand of it.

* * * * *

The age in which we now live is characterized by an assortment of illogical, theology-denying statements. For example, it is quite possible that you could have a conversation with someone who would say to you:

> There is no such thing as absolute truth. Therefore, your Christian faith rests on a foundation based on unfounded hopes and dreams.

In response to such a declaration, I would simply ask, "Are you sure of that?" If the person says, "Yes," I then would ask: "Aren't you making a statement of 'absolute truth'—the very thing that you claim doesn't exist?"

When this happens in conversation, it generally shows the illogical nature of the original statement. Of course, that same person could parrot something that Jones might say, declaring:

> The only truth is change itself. Therefore, your Christian doctrines are also subject to change.

I would then counter with this: "Is your statement also subject to change? If it is, then why do you bother to even say it?"

These examples are only a small sampling of the multiple challenges to Christian theology that confront us today. Even Pope Francis has weighed in, claiming that fundamentalism— strongly held religious convictions—closes the door to real humanity:

- Religious fundamentalism keeps God at a distance, and keeps believers from building bridges with others, Pope Francis reflected on Sunday during a radio interview (Catholic News Agency).

Meanwhile, Scripture informs us that God encourages us to believe certain fundamentals of the faith. For example:

- "For God so loved the world that he gave his one and only Son, that whoever believes in him shall not perish but have eternal life. For God did not send his Son into the world to condemn the world, but to save the world through him" (John 3:16-17).

Are we Christians not supposed to be assured by the fundamental truth that Christ died for our sins and, on the basis of that truth, know that we have peace with God?

However, it seems that, according to Francis, a fundamental truth like this would only "…divert [our] minds from him."

- "Our God is a God who is close, who accompanies. Fundamentalists keep God away from accompanying his people; they divert their minds from him and transform him into an ideology. So in the name of this ideological god, they kill, they attack, destroy, slander. Practically-speaking, they transform that God into a Baal, an idol" (Catholic News Agency).

I had no idea that my knowledge of the fundamental truth found in John 3:16 would, as Francis says, "keep God away"!

Although I have much more growing to do in the area of loving others, it is doctrinal and theological truth—coupled with the truth of my utter unworthiness apart from Him—that draws me lovingly to those I would ordinarily hate.

In point of fact, it is these same Christian fundamentals that deflate my arrogance, my sense of entitlement, and humble me to follow Jesus. It is these truths that have motivated me to reach out in friendship and to forgive those who hurt me.

Why do I do these things? I do them because of another fundamental truth found in the Bible: I must forgive as I have been forgiven.

Of course, it matters what fundamentals we embrace.

If world conquest is the fundamental or ideal, then that will have a stifling effect on the way I reach out to others in friendship. If violent socialistic revolution, for another example, is the fundamental, then chaos and destruction are guaranteed. People would be considered mere objects to be manipulated for the achieving of the final goal.

However, if love and justice—two of the cornerstones of biblical theology—are our fundamentals, then real peace will be the fruit.

Works Cited

Jones, Tony. *The New Christians*. Jossey-Bass, 2008.

Nozaki, Warren. "Paradise Still Lost in Eckhart Tolle's 'A New Earth.'" *Christian Research Journal*, vol. 31, no. 5, 2008.

"For Pope Francis, Religious Fundamentalism Diverts Us from the True God." *Catholic News Agency,* 16 September 2015, www.catholicnewsagency.com/news/for-pope-francis-religious-fundamentalism-diverts-us-from-the-true-god-16824/. Accessed 26 September 2016.

Chapter 3

MYSTICAL EXPERIENCES AND TECHNIQUES: SHOULD CHRISTIANS GET ON BOARD?

CHAPTER SUMMARY
Many complain that doctrine divides us and deprives us of the unity necessary to heal the world's divisions. These same people claim that common mystical experiences that are available to all religious groups can bring us together. However, this hope is entirely unbiblical.

Theology is no longer relevant.

After all, many in the Western church are choosing mystical experience over doctrinal truth. Why is this? They insist that doctrines divide us, while common mystical experiences can bring us together.

Mysticism is now touted as the means to directly experience God, making our "divisive" doctrines unnecessary. These experiences are achieved, not through believing the truth or even living the truth, but through techniques available to all, irrespective of one's religious orientation.

In this regard, sociologist Tony Campolo writes:

- "A theology of mysticism provides some hope for common ground between Christianity and Islam. Both religions have within their histories examples of ecstatic union with God...I do not know what to make of the

Muslim mystics, especially those who have come to be known as the Sufis. What do they experience in their mystical experiences? Could they have encountered the same God we do in our Christian mysticism?" (Oakland 108)

According to Campolo, we can plug into God through mystical techniques and experiences, and then, this shared experience can become the basis for a "common ground" among the various religions.

Campolo claims that he has been able to achieve what he calls intimacy with Christ through "centering prayer" (Oakland 113). For him, this involves the repetition of the name of Jesus. However, he suggests that Muslims—and, by extension, others—may also be able to achieve this same "intimacy with Christ" through the use of similar mystical techniques.

If what Campolo says is true, then theology and doctrine are no longer important or even necessary. After all, wouldn't Christian ideology serve only to build walls and present obstacles to obtaining this union with God?

This most assuredly raises the question: "What exactly is this 'ecstatic union with God'?" The plain truth here is that the Bible makes no mention of such a thing. This biblical silence speaks all the more loudly in light of the fact that Scripture claims to provide everything that we need for a relationship with God:

- All Scripture is God-breathed and is useful for teaching, rebuking, correcting and training in righteousness, so that the man of God may be thoroughly equipped for every good work (2 Timothy 3:16-17).

If the so-called common ground of mysticism and "ecstatic union with God" are the means by which the world's religions lead us all into a time of unity and peace, we should expect that the Bible would have something to say about it. However, Scripture insists that, for spiritual matters, "Do not go beyond what is written" (I Corinthians 4:6; Isaiah 8:19-20).

If anyone had experienced an "ecstatic union with God," it was Jesus on the Mount of Transfiguration. And if there was ever a teachable moment to introduce mystical methods, this would certainly have been it.

However, instead of teaching His disciples about how they too might have this sort of ecstatic union, Jesus, in Matthew 17:11, instructed them *not to tell anyone about what they had seen!*

Moses also had a fantastic mountain-top experience in which his countenance was transformed. However, instead of telling the Israelites about how they also could experience God in this way, he directed them to God's *words* (Exodus 34:29-34). Rather than focusing on having an experience with God, Moses placed the emphasis upon the Word of God.

Tony Campolo and other similarly-minded people fail to recognize that there is a prohibitive price to be paid for genuine experiences or revelations from God. The Apostle Paul had the amazing experience of being taken up into heaven. However, in order that he not become proud about what he had learned and experienced, God chastened him severely (2 Corinthians 12:1-10).

As we continue to discuss this matter, it is important for us to recognize that each one of these transformative experiences we see in the Bible was the product of *God's initiative and not human manipulation*. In fact, the idea that we humans can coerce an "ecstatic union with God" is sheer arrogance.

At a low point in his ministry, Moses requested a divine revelation: "Show me your glory" (Exodus 33:18). However, God delivered His answer in the form of doctrinal content rather than an ecstatic experience. Placing Moses in the cleft of a rock while His glory passed by, God honored His servant with these Self-disclosures:

- And he said [to Moses], "I will make all my goodness pass before you and will proclaim before you my name 'The LORD.' And I will be gracious to whom I will be gracious, and will show mercy on whom I will show mercy" (Exodus 33:19).

- The LORD passed before him and proclaimed, "The LORD, the LORD, a God merciful and gracious, slow to anger, and abounding in steadfast love and faithfulness" (Exodus 34:6).

So we see that, yet again, doctrinal content trumps ecstatic experience.

There is another issue that needs to be addressed here: What assurance do practitioners of mystical techniques have that they aren't plugging into something malevolent?

Mystic Richard Foster claims…

- …that practitioners must use caution. He admits that in contemplative prayer "we are entering deeply into the spiritual realm," and that sometimes it is not the realm of God, even though it is "supernatural." He admits there are spiritual beings and that a prayer of protection should be said beforehand—something to the effect of "All dark and evil spirits must now leave" (Oakland 99).

Foster is presumptuous if he thinks that a mere "prayer of protection" will suffice. In view of these spiritual threats, he should be asking whether or not he has taken the wrong path, an unbiblical one that has taken him outside the jurisdiction of God's protective hand.

Keeping in mind that—according to 2 Corinthians 11:14—the Devil poses as an agent of the light, what guarantee does Foster have that he hasn't been deceived?

This leads us to the next question: "Can people of other religions employ mystical techniques to experience God?"

To answer this, Scripture is clear: God would be the last Person that the unredeemed would want to experience. A glance at Romans 8:6-7 would show us that, naturally-speaking, we hate God and can't stand His presence.

The Apostle John knew this to be true:

- "This is the verdict: Light has come into the world, but men loved darkness instead of light because their deeds were evil. Everyone who does evil hates the light, and will not come into the light for fear that his deeds will be exposed" (John 3:19-20).

Even the children of Israel could not tolerate God's presence:

- When the people saw the thunder and lightning and heard the trumpet and saw the mountain in smoke, they trembled with fear. They stayed at a distance and said to Moses, "Speak to us yourself and we will listen. But do not have God speak to us or we will die" (Exodus 20:18-19).

The last thing the Israelites wanted was a more intimate encounter!

Surprisingly, God was pleased that Israel had this fearful awareness and, therefore, wouldn't try to pursue a mystical union with Him. As it turns out, the feeling was mutual. Before the redemption that was secured on the Cross, God did not want to be in Israel's presence either. He explained that He might destroy the Israelites if He came into their presence:

- "I will send an angel before you and drive out the Canaanites, Amorites, Hittites, Perizzites, Hivites and Jebusites. Go up to the land flowing with milk and honey. But I will not go with you, because you are a stiff-necked people and I might destroy you on the way" (Exodus 33:2- 3).

What does Foster do with verses like these?

Returning once again to the Tony Campolo quotation at the beginning of this chapter, we find that he suggests that the Muslims might also be connecting with "God" through their mystical experiences...*apart from faith in Christ.* However, if they were to experience God, the reality is that they would be experiencing His wrath:

- The wrath of God is being revealed from heaven against all the godlessness and wickedness of men who suppress the truth by their wickedness (Romans 1:18).

It is only through faith in Jesus that we have been redeemed from the wrath of God. It is only through Him that we can enter boldly into His presence:

- Therefore, brothers, since we have confidence to enter the Most Holy Place by the blood of Jesus, by a new and living way opened for us through the curtain, that is, his body, and since we have a great priest over the house of God, let us draw near to God with a sincere heart in full assurance of faith, having our hearts sprinkled to cleanse us from a guilty conscience and having our bodies washed with pure water (Hebrews 10:19-22).

Mysticism would not be quite so provocative if it only claimed to influence our personal experience. However, *it also claims to influence God!*

Here is something else that Campolo wrote:

- "The constant repetition of his name clears my head of everything but the awareness of his presence. By driving back all other concerns, I am able to create what the ancient Celtic Christians called 'the thin place.' The thin place is that spiritual condition wherein the separation between the self and God becomes so thin that God is able to break through and envelope the soul" (Oakland 114).

Mr. Campolo claims that, through the constant repetition of God's name, he can create some sort of atmospheric thin space wherein this less-than-omnipotent "God" is thus enabled to "break through and envelope the soul." In essence, this makes Campolo the prime agent of communication here, since God— without Tony's help—was not able to bridge that gap!

However, Scripture assures us that God already lives within us to such an extent that we can confidently say:

- I have been crucified with Christ and I no longer live, but Christ lives in me (Galatians 2:20).

Mysticism preaches a different Christ, one who is not omnipotent and cannot break through to us without our mindless repetitions or other profane techniques.

Besides this, Scripture does not teach us that we need to create a "thin place" so that God can break through. Instead, as David assured us, every place is a "thin place" for our God:

- The LORD is my shepherd; I shall not want. He makes me lie down in green pastures. He leads me beside still waters. He restores my soul. He leads me in paths of righteousness for his name's sake. Even though I walk through the valley of the shadow of death, I will fear no evil, for you are with me; your rod and your staff, they comfort me (Psalm 23:1-4).

Moreover, Jesus warned us specifically against practicing vain and meaningless repetitions:

- "And when you pray, do not keep on babbling like pagans, for they think they will be heard because of their many words" (Matthew 6:7).

Repeating words and phrases might make us feel connected, but in actuality, such practices have nothing to do with our relationship with our Savior. Instead, God wants truth—not a preoccupation with repeated words—in our hearts:

- Surely you desire truth in the inner parts; you teach me wisdom in the inmost place (Psalm 51:6).

This truth should entail contrition and repentance and not ecstatic union!

Returning once again to perhaps the most troubling of all the comments we have examined here is this: Tony Campolo claims that, through his "centering prayer," *he* is the one who has removed or thinned the separating barrier between God and himself. However, God claims that this is a barrier that *He* has eliminated through the Cross, splitting in two the veil that separated the people from the presence of God in the temple:

- And when Jesus had cried out again in a loud voice, he gave up his spirit. At that moment the curtain of the temple was torn in two from top to bottom. The earth shook and the rocks split (Matthew 27:50-51).

Of course, this is not to deny that we do indeed erect barriers through our sins. However, we confront such barriers through confession and repentance, *not mystical practices!*

In general, the mystics teach a different Christ, a Christ who is not so much concerned about truth, faith, doctrine, righteousness, repentance, obedience, and holiness. Instead, as they see things, God is more concerned that we learn the proper techniques— repetitions, centering prayers, using our imagination, visualizations, and practicing silence.

Unfortunately for the mystics, these are practices that find absolutely no biblical support.

Experience is essential to the Christian life, but we can enjoy and appreciate our experiences through the blessing of learning about our Lord:

- Grace and peace be yours in abundance *through the knowledge of God and of Jesus our Lord.* His divine power has given us everything we need for life and godliness *through our knowledge of him who called us by his own glory and goodness* (2 Peter 1:2-3, emphasis added).

Here is truth we can exult in:

- This is what the LORD says:
  "Let not the wise man boast of his wisdom
          or the strong man boast of his strength
          or the rich man boast of his riches,
      but let him who boasts boast about this:
          that he understands and knows me,
      that I am the LORD, who exercises kindness,

justice and righteousness on earth,
for in these I delight,"
declares the LORD.
Jeremiah 9:23-24

Our experiences and feelings reflect what we understand. Having experienced decades of depression and self-loathing prior to coming to Christ, these tendencies were deeply engraved in my flesh. They were so deep that I felt that God actually loathed me. It seemed to me in my twisted way of thinking that God had created humanity for His own sadistic entertainment—and there was plenty about which He could laugh.

However, one evening, He made very real for me the Cross, His own suffering, and His compassion (Hebrews 4:15; Isaiah 63:9). My tears of gratitude have not yet ceased to flow!

SOMETIMES, DIVISIONS ARE UNAVOIDABLE, EVEN NECESSARY...

In the Church, we are to avoid divisions. The Apostle Paul pleaded with us, that we would maintain our unity:

- Be completely humble and gentle; be patient, bearing with one another in love. Make every effort to keep the unity of the Spirit through the bond of peace. There is one body and one Spirit—just as you were called to one hope when you were called—one Lord, one faith, one baptism; one God and Father of all, who is over all and through all and in all (Ephesians 4:2-6).

However, we can only preserve unity where there is already a basis or foundation—Jesus—for that unity. Just as a skilled midwife is not able to bring forth a baby where none exists in the womb, we in the Church are not able to create bonds of fellowship where there is no existing spiritual brotherhood. That would be like trying to create some sort of bond between a snake and a rodent.

Rather, we are called to be separate from the world:

- Do not be yoked together with unbelievers. For what do righteousness and wickedness have in common? Or what fellowship can light have with darkness? What harmony is there between Christ and Belial? What does a believer have in common with an unbeliever? What agreement is there between the temple of God and idols? For we are the temple of the living God (2 Corinthians 6:14-16a).

It is Christ's unity that must be preserved and not a unity of our own invention. We must not compromise our relationship with the Savior in bonds of "fellowship" that will lead us into compromise.

This does not mean that we cannot love and befriend those who do not also profess Christ. We certainly must. But these bonds must not diminish the life we have in the Lord.

We cannot be yoked together with unbelievers in a way that compromises the relationship we have with our Bridegroom, Christ. And in this "marriage," we must be scrupulous about anything that might harm His bride, the Body of Christ. "A little leaven [sin] leavens [corrupts] the whole loaf" (Galatians 5:9).

In the book of Revelation, the Holy Spirit provided the seven churches of Asia Minor with the results of His theological evaluation. It might come as a surprise to some people that the church at Ephesus was commended for its intolerance and willingness to risk divisions:

- "I know your deeds, your hard work and your perseverance. I know that you cannot tolerate wicked men, that you have tested those who claim to be apostles but are not, and have found them false. You have persevered and have endured hardships for my name, and have not grown weary" (Revelation 2:2-3).

Sometimes intolerance and division are commendable in the life of a church. There are even some situations when excommunication must be implemented.

When we continue to study the book of Revelation, we find that there were times when the churches were too tolerant, too concerned about achieving an unbiblical and superficial unity. For this error in judgment, one of the churches was castigated by the Spirit. This was the case with the church at Pergamum:

- "Nevertheless, I have a few things against you: You have people there who hold to the teaching of Balaam, who taught Balak to entice the Israelites to sin by eating food sacrificed to idols and by committing sexual immorality. Likewise you also have those who hold to the teaching of the Nicolaitans. Repent therefore!" (Revelation 2:14-16)

Evidently, the church at Pergamum lacked an adequate understanding or appreciation for God's truths and concerns—theology!

This was also the case with the church at Thyatira:

- "Nevertheless, I have this against you: You tolerate that woman Jezebel, who calls herself a prophetess. By her teaching she misleads my servants into sexual immorality and the eating of food sacrificed to idols. I have given her time to repent of her immorality, but she is unwilling" (Revelation 2:20-21).

Excommunication seems so archaic, intolerant and unloving to modern ears. However, we are instructed to pursue this form of discipline, not only for the benefit of the Church, but also for the miscreant. Paul mentions two such offenders:

- Timothy... fight the good fight, holding on to faith and a good conscience. Some have rejected these and so have shipwrecked their faith. Among them are Hymenaeus and Alexander, whom I have handed over to Satan to be taught not to blaspheme (1 Timothy 1:18-20).

For their own welfare, Hymenaeus and Alexander had to be taught not to blaspheme. To accomplish this, the strong judgment of excommunication was meted out with the hope that it would bring about repentance.

Excommunication was also advised for an unrepentant man who was having sex with his father's wife:

- When you are assembled in the name of our Lord Jesus and I am with you in spirit, and the power of our Lord Jesus is present, hand this man over to Satan, so that the sinful nature may be destroyed and his spirit saved on the day of the Lord (1 Corinthians 5:4-5).

From these examples we can see that Paul was concerned, not only for the Church, but also for the salvation of the unrepentant.

We Christians are often told: "You should not judge."

However, when our critics judge us in this manner, they are being hypocritical, since they too are judging. This is just one more proof that demonstrates that there is no way around judging and making decisions about any number of issues. To judge is a necessary part of life.

Finally, can mystical experience unite the world and bring the peace for which Tony Campolo hopes? I don't see how. Even now, Christians and non-Christians alike already share many common experiences, such as fear, desire, family, children, friends, anxiety—the list is almost endless. However, none of these commonalities that we share has brought peace. Why then should we expect that *another* common experience—using certain mystical techniques—would give us peace?

My wife and I share many common experiences. However, it is essential that we both strive to maintain peace.

How do we do this? With God's theological truths! These pearls of wisdom from the Word offer us detailed instructions about how we can please God and love others:

- Do not let any unwholesome talk come out of your mouths, but only what is helpful for building others up according to their needs, that it may benefit those who listen. And do not grieve the Holy Spirit of God, with whom you were sealed for the day of redemption. Get rid of all bitterness, rage and anger, brawling and slander, along with every form of malice. Be kind and compassionate to one another, forgiving each other, just as in Christ God forgave you (Ephesians 4:29-32).

These truths take precedence over all our feelings, all our experiences, and any "techniques" we might be tempted to investigate and learn. I believe that when we get our theology right, over the course of time, everything else in life will fall into its rightful place, just as God intended it!

Works Cited

Oakland, Roger. *Faith Undone*. Lighthouse Trails Publishing, 2007.

Chapter 4

THEOLOGY: IS CERTAINTY POSSIBLE?

CHAPTER SUMMARY

The claim that we cannot be certain about our faith is another roadblock to theology. This is the position of the Emergent and Postmodern churches and their spokesmen, like Brian McLaren. However, this embrace of uncertainty is illogical, unbiblical, and life-denying.

In case you haven't noticed, we live in a strange and mixed-up world.

Uncertainty has become a reigning virtue and a hindrance to theology. After all, how can we confidently say anything certain about our faith if such certainty is impossible?

Therefore, according to this world-view, the "truth" of uncertainty leaves us only one option—a blind leap into the darkness of faith. And, if our faith is indeed blind, then it follows that this state of blindness should discourage us from telling anyone that it is the truth!

Sandy Ikeda is a professor of economics at Purchase College, SUNY. He is understandably troubled by the religious and sectarian violence perpetrated by those who are *certain* that they are right:

- Today in the Ukraine, in Gaza and Israel, in Syria, in South Sudan, and in far too many other places around the world, deadly violence ruins lives and sickens the heart (Ikeda).

And this violence should sicken the heart. However, Ikeda goes on to identify *certainty* as one of the contributing problems:

- For what it's worth, in my religious tradition there's a saying: *Nothing is what you think it is.* Because of the narrowness and limits of our perceptions, there's an inevitable disconnect between what we think we know about the world and the way things actually are, between what we see and what is actually the case. That, of course, causes problems. But it gets much worse if we refuse even to acknowledge that the disjunction exists, and if we cling to the belief that in at least some part of our belief system we are absolutely, unshakably right. The more certain we feel about what we know, and the more we think we're certain about, the worse it gets (Ikeda).

It is true that certainty about things that do not warrant our certainty—like certainty about that which is false—is definitely a problem. Yet, we should not make the mistake of rejecting all forms of certainty because of the dangers inherent in only some kinds of it. In fact, only by having certainty can we reject the dangerous varieties of certainty.

For example, without being certain about the goodness of truth, love and justice, we cannot say that genocide is absolutely wrong. Nor would we be able to take meaningful action against it.

To deny any degree of certainty narrows and degrades our lives. It reduces us from truth-seekers to mere experience-seekers. Such a stance downgrades the necessary decision-making in our lives to a matter of merely how we feel.

To illustrate this, let's consider a simple example. If you are mugged, should you go to the police?

The answer to that question depends on what you believe about justice and human culpability. If you do not know what to believe about those issues or objective moral guilt, you will not be certain about what action to take. Your uncertainty will leave you in a confused state. And besides that, your inaction will make your neighbors vulnerable because a mugger is running free.

These concerns are not simply matters of ivory-tower philosophizing; they affect us right where we live, in all of our daily lives.

Of course, there are many areas of legitimate uncertainty. For example, none of us knows what is going to happen tomorrow. But that does not mean that every area of our lives needs to be clouded by uncertainty.

For years, I was plagued by doubts about the existence of God and whether He really loved me. I am glad that I never resigned myself to the belief that certainty about these concerns was not possible. If we have no confidence that we are loved by God, we will crave the love and approval of others. We might even go so far as to resent people if we don't receive their unqualified approval.

This is why it is so important for us to recognize that certainty about the Gospel of Christ is of the highest importance. In fact, this was the central issue of John's letter to the Church:

- We know that we have come to know him if we keep his commands. Whoever says, "I know him," but does not do what he commands is a liar, and the truth is not in that person. But if anyone obeys his word, love for God is truly made complete in them. This is how we know we are in him…(1 John 2:3-5)

We can be certain and KNOW that we are in Him by whether or not we keep His commandments.

* * * * *

Meanwhile, many in the Emergent, or Postmodern, Church insist that certainty about God—theological certainty—is not possible. Pastor Brian McLaren reflects this skepticism when he claims that, among other things, we can never be certain about our interpretation of Scripture:

- "How do 'I' know the Bible is always right? And if 'I' am sophisticated enough to realize that I know nothing of the Bible without my own involvement via interpretation, I'll also ask how I know which school, method, or technique of biblical interpretation is right. What makes a 'good' interpretation good? And if an appeal is made to a written standard (book, doctrinal statement, etc.) or to common sense or to 'scholarly principles of interpretation,' the same pesky 'I' who liberated us from the authority of the church will ask, 'Who sets the standard? Whose common sense? Which scholars and why? Don't all these appeals to authorities and principles outside the Bible actually undermine the claim of ultimate biblical authority? Aren't they just the new pope?'" (DeWaay)

McLaren inflates the problems of interpretation. Irrationally, he claims that he is *certain* that we cannot interpret Scripture with any degree of certainty without first having a proven method of interpretation. How ironic that, while McLaren denies that we can be certain, his many books declare that *he* is certain about a number of things!

A little common sense plus a handful of experience might shed some light on this "problem" of acquiring certainty.

We engage in easy-to-understand conversations all the time, without a proven system of interpretation. When I ask the attendant to pump me $20 of "regular," he knows exactly what to do. There's no confusion; no need for a proven method of interpretation. Why should it be any different when interpreting the Bible?

When I read the "50 mph" speed limit sign on the highway, I would like to believe that it means "65 mph." However, I *know* what it means. In fact, this interpretation is further confirmed when the highway patrol tickets me for doing "65." Interpretation does not pose any significant problems, except for those who are trying to derive an interpretation which the text—or speed limit sign—cannot support.

Likewise, there are numerous ways to verify our interpretation of Scripture. Any one particular verse can have many corroborating verses. We call this "Scripture interpreting Scripture."

Of course, some passages in the Bible—for example, 2 Peter 3:15—can be difficult to understand. But this does not mean that much of what is written is not quite plain. Besides, we have many other aids—pastors, teachers, commentaries, concordances—to help us understand.

We need to remember the simple fact that Scripture was written to be understood. Therefore, Paul made it abundantly clear that his epistles were to be delivered to and read in multiple congregations of the Early Church. It is worth noting that he never insisted that a Doctor of Theology be present to provide the definitive interpretation.

None of the Apostles ever suggested that those who listened to them were required to have a proven system of interpretation before apostolic teaching could be understood.

If McLaren had written that *much* of Scripture presents us with interpretative difficulties, many of us would agree. However, he is skeptical about *all* interpretations of Scripture. If only he were equally as skeptical about his own conclusions!

* * * * *

In recent years, it has become fashionable for a fair share of the populace to believe that people cannot be sure of anything regarding biblical faith.

Confirming this mind-set, Brian McLaren asks: "How do 'I' know the Bible is always right?" The way he frames the question suggests that none of us can know.

One noted theologian wrote:

- Any worldview—atheist, Islamic, Jewish, Christian or whatever—ultimately depends on assumptions that cannot be proved. Every house is built on foundations, and the foundations of worldviews are not ultimately capable of being proved in every respect.

However, such a stance is logically self-defeating. If it is true that we believe as we do based simply on blind and baseless faith, then the above statement is also a matter of blind faith and therefore, it disqualifies itself.

The most potent defense against this irrational thinking is that the Bible itself disqualifies uncertainty!

Many verses contend that there is evidence that serves as an incontestable basis for an assured faith:

- Then the LORD said to Moses: "How long will these people reject me? And how long will they not believe me,

with all the signs which I have performed among them?"
(Numbers 14:11, emphasis added)

According to Moses, there was no excuse for Israel's uncertainty and unbelief:

- Or has any god ever attempted to go and take a nation for himself from the midst of another nation, by trials, by signs, by wonders, and by war, by a mighty hand and an outstretched arm, and by great deeds of terror, all of which the LORD your God did for you in Egypt before your eyes? To you it was shown, *that you might know that the LORD is God; there is no other besides him* (Deuteronomy 4:34-35, emphasis added).

In addition, God made certain truths, like the resurrection, abundantly certain:

- After his suffering, he presented himself to them *and gave many convincing proofs that he was alive*. He appeared to them over a period of forty days and spoke about the kingdom of God (Acts 1:3, emphasis added).

God never dismisses the questions and honest doubts of His people by admonishing them and saying, "Just believe." Instead, He has provided many unassailable proofs for the faith.

This does not mean that we don't struggle with doubts and uncertainties. Nor does it mean that these challenges are harmful to the faith and therefore must be suppressed. Nor does it mean that God cannot bring great good out of such struggles. He does this again and again.

However, the Emergent, Postmodern, skeptical Church places too much emphasis on the journey and the search. There is just a minimal stress on the object or goal of the search—certainty and assurance regarding biblical truth.

Emergents have normalized and idealized the journey at the expense of the cognitive rest and assurance that can be found at the end of the search. They even claim—with arrogance, in my opinion—that assurance is possible only for those who do not think deeply about things.

When I think about my own journey, I admit that faith was a struggle for me. I was weak in faith and rich in skepticism.

It tormented me that I could find no peace in believing. To make matters worse, it seemed to me that others had found the peace I so desperately craved. I therefore would have welcomed the Emergent message that certainty isn't possible. It would have given me some satisfaction to know that I had something in common with other highly-educated believers. I wouldn't have felt like such a Christian misfit.

Fortunately, I found little encouragement that skepticism would be my ultimate resting place, the goal of my searching.

Instead, I learned that joyously living the Christian life is not possible without a high degree of certainty. I needed to know that God loved me with a love that transcended understanding (Ephesians 3:16-19). I needed to know that He had forgiven and cleansed me from all of my sins. In short, I absolutely needed the confidence that is mentioned so often throughout Scripture:

- Therefore, brothers and sisters, *since we have confidence* to enter the Most Holy Place by the blood of Jesus, by a new and living way opened for us through the curtain, that is, his body, and since we have a great priest over the house of God, let us draw near to God with a sincere heart *and with the full assurance that faith brings*, having our hearts sprinkled to cleanse us from a guilty conscience and having our bodies washed with pure water (Hebrews 10:19-22, emphasis added).

We require confidence so that we can draw close to our Savior and know that He has drawn close to us.

As long as I doubted His love, I could not feel grateful towards Him. In fact, I felt contempt for Him, not knowing with certainty that He truly loved me. Whenever I felt reproved by my feelings, I also felt that God was censuring me. I needed to know for sure that He wasn't condemning me and that my feelings were only feelings, and not reality.

And that is the very place where Scripture comforted me:

- Therefore, there is now no condemnation for those who are in Christ Jesus (Romans 8:1).

With the certainty that this new knowledge brought me, I was able to fully embrace and rejoice in Paul's prayer for the Church:

- I pray that you, being rooted and established in love, may have power, together with all the Lord's holy people, to grasp how wide and long and high and deep is the love of Christ, *and to know this love that surpasses knowledge*—that you may be filled to the measure of all the fullness of God (Ephesians 3:17-19, emphasis added).

Having the assurance of the knowledge of God and His love for us is not an option. Without this knowledge, we will not be "filled to the measure of all the fullness of God." Without this confidence, we will not be able to persevere:

- So do not throw away your confidence; it will be richly rewarded. You need to persevere so that when you have done the will of God, you will receive what he has promised (Hebrews 10:35-36).

Without confidence in the promises of God, I was simply not able to persevere. Now that I have this confidence, I must confess...I still struggle. And yet, because of what He has shown me from His Word, God has enabled me to continue to move forward in my life. I am certain of His truth, no matter how I might be feeling.

Finally, it is worth noting that Paul associated knowledge with rejoicing, or glorying:

- We also glory in our sufferings, because we know that suffering produces perseverance (Romans 5:3).

Without this knowledge—and the confidence that it brings—we cannot glory in suffering. But with this knowledge, we can rejoice in the midst of suffering because we are confident that God has a glorious purpose for it (Romans 8:28).

When I did not have this confidence, I suffered from obsessive, crippling ruminations:

> *Does God love me? Is He disgusted by me? Has He left me? Am I a spiritual failure? Will I always be one?*

Now, with my shield of faith in place, I can confidently face down these doubts and even laugh at them. How can I do this?

I can do this now because—through His Word—I *know* who my God is!

* * * * *

Doubting Thomas could have told the skeptics in the Church today something about certainty. He had doubted that Jesus had risen from the dead. Then, Jesus visited him and showed him the wounds in His hands and side (John 20). After Jesus proved Himself to Thomas, he worshiped Christ with all the certainty in the world.

The lesson is very simple: our Lord is well able to remove doubt and provide assurance for His children. The need for theological certainty is vital for our lives.

It was only because of the certainty that Christ gave him that Thomas was enabled to carry the Gospel to far-off India and to his eventual martyrdom.

It is only with the certainty that God gives us through our knowledge of the Word that we are enabled to live our lives in Christ…and to face whatever He has in store for us.

Works Cited

DeWaay, Bob. "Emergent Delusion: A Critique of Brian McLaren, A Generous Orthodoxy." *Critical Issues Commentary*, March/April 2005, www.cicministry.org/commentary/issue87.htm. Accessed 20 November 2015.

Ikeda, Sandy. "Violence and the Illusion of Certainty." *Foundation for Economic Education*, 4 September 2014, fee.org/articles/violence-and-the-illusion-of-certainty/. Accessed November 2015.

Chapter 5

FAITH:
IS BIBLICAL FAITH BLIND?

CHAPTER SUMMARY
Faith is neither devoid of understanding or evidence.
Richard Dawkins and others insist that it is, but this is not
what the Bible teaches about faith. Instead, faith entails
both understanding and evidence.

According to atheist and evolutionist Richard Dawkins, biblical faith represents the rejection of evidence and rationality:

- Faith is the great cop-out, the great excuse to evade the need to think and evaluate evidence. Faith is belief in spite of, even perhaps because of, the lack of evidence (Dawkins).

However, this is not the Bible's idea of faith.

Faith is not a blind leap into the abyss of mindlessness, but a willingness to step forth into the light of evidence. This is the consistent message of Scripture.

When God asked Israel to love and obey Him, He never intended Israel to follow Him like a dumb beast. Instead, He asked the Israelites to *remember the gracious miracles that they had all witnessed:*

- Has any god ever tried to take for himself one nation out of another nation, by testings, by miraculous signs and wonders, by war, by a mighty hand and an outstretched arm, or by great and awesome deeds, like all the things the LORD your God did for you in Egypt before your very eyes? You were shown these things so that you might know that the LORD is God; besides him there is no other (Deuteronomy 4:34-35).

Faith does not require a mental lobotomy. In fact, this is expressly forbidden. According to Deuteronomy 19:15, everything had to be confirmed by witnesses. This is why Jesus advised His disciples not to believe in Him... *if He did not provide confirmatory evidence:*

- "Do not believe me unless I do what my Father does" (John 10:37).

- "If I [alone] testify about myself, my testimony is not valid" (John 5:31).

Therefore, Jesus provided one proof after another to confirm the validity of His ministry and His teachings:

- "Even though you do not believe me, believe the miracles, that you may know and understand that the Father is in me, and I in the Father" (John 10:38).

- "I am telling you now before it happens, so that when it does happen you will believe that I am He" (John 13:19; 14:28-29).

- "If I had not done among them what no one else did, they would not be guilty of sin. But now they have seen these miracles, and yet they have hated both me and my Father" (John 15:24).

According to Jesus, ignorance is a good excuse. However, His contemporaries were not ignorant of His miracles. They had seen them; therefore, they were culpable.

The Christian faith depends upon reasons for that faith. Jesus' disciples had abandoned Him after the crucifixion. They were convinced that their faith had been for naught, despite the many miracles they had witnessed. They were on the run—until Jesus' miraculous resurrection appearances turned them back:

- After his suffering, he showed himself to these men and gave many convincing proofs that he was alive. He appeared to them over a period of forty days and spoke about the kingdom of God (Acts 1:3).

It was these "proofs" that revived the faith of Jesus' disciples. In fact, an overwhelming abundance of proof and evidence provided an absolutely essential foundation for their faith.

Surprisingly, there are a number of Christians who claim that the Bible is not about proof, but proclamation. Actually, the Bible is about *both* proof and proclamation.

As we examine Peter's sermon on the day of Pentecost, we can see that the evidentiary proofs concerning Christ's ministry were undeniable:

- "Men of Israel, listen to this: Jesus of Nazareth was a man accredited by God to you by miracles, wonders and signs, which God did among you through him, as you yourselves know" (Acts 2:22).

Despite the wealth of biblical evidence that God indeed has provided proof and a sure foundation for our faith, some Christians are still convinced that faith is blind. They sometimes defend this stance by citing two verses—erroneously—in support of their contention. Let's take a look…

After Jesus appeared to doubting Thomas, he believed and worshiped Him. However, the Lord rebuked Thomas:

- Then Jesus told him, "Because you have seen me, you have believed; blessed are those who have not seen and yet have believed" (John 20:29).

Some Christians wrongly understand this verse to mean…*blessed are those who believe without any evidence.* Such a misunderstanding of interpretation represents a failure to appreciate the context of Jesus' words. Actually, there was an abundance of evidence!

Let us carefully consider the following:

1. Everyone was aware of Jesus' miracles, even His detractors. In many passages, the Jewish Talmud acknowledges that Jesus was a miracle-worker. The miracles are ascribed to Satan, but those who wrote the Talmud acknowledged that they did actually take place.

2. Thomas had lived with Jesus for two or three years and had seen many of His miracles—perhaps hundreds of them. In addition, Thomas had the testimonial evidence of his fellow disciples, who claimed that they had seen Jesus after His resurrection. Therefore, Thomas had an abundance of evidence to believe that Christ had risen from the dead. A lack of proof was certainly not the root of his problem.

3. A very important component of Thomas' story, often overlooked, is this: Thomas was not simply seeking evidence of the resurrection—*he was demanding to see it:*

   - So the other disciples told him, "We have seen the Lord!" But he said to them, "Unless I see the nail marks in his hands and put my finger where the nails were, and put my hand into his side, I will not believe it" (John 20:25).

51

The disciples had claimed that they had seen Jesus. However, Thomas refused to accept their testimonies. Instead, he obstinately demanded that he also might actually see the risen Christ, despite the fact that he already had plenty of evidence.

In view of this, when Jesus affirmed the blessedness of "those who have not seen and yet have believed," He was affirming the willingness of the disciples to believe without making demands of seeing for themselves, as Thomas had done.

The notion that Jesus would praise those who had faith *without any solid reasons for their faith* contradicts all of Scripture! It even contradicts the very next verse in the passage:

- Jesus did many other miraculous signs in the presence of his disciples, which are not recorded in this book. But these are written that you may believe that Jesus is the Christ, the Son of God, and that by believing you may have life in his name (John 20:30-31).

John acknowledges here that belief should be accompanied by reasons to believe.

Although the great majority of John's readers had not seen the resurrection, this should not be viewed as any sort of a stumbling block to prevent faith. According to John, there was plenty of other evidence for faith—namely, the testimonial proofs that John and other eyewitnesses had provided.

It is highly unlikely that John would have written against an evidence-based faith—and then go on to offer copious evidence in his Gospel "…that [they] may believe."

Some Christians cite a second, very familiar verse to prove that faith is a mindless, evidence-less plunge into non-rationality:

- Now faith is being sure of what we hope for and certain of what we do not see (Hebrews 11:1).

This verse says nothing against an evidence-based faith. Even if faith is our *only* assurance—and it is not—faith is not devoid of evidential reasons, whether they be objective or very personal.

For example, the Apostles had faith in Jesus because He gave them reasons for their faith—an evidential foundation.

Similarly, the Samaritan woman at the well had faith because Jesus had given her a basis for her faith, which she declared to the other Samaritans:

- Many Samaritans from that town believed in him because of the woman's testimony, "He told me all that I ever did" (John 4:39).

Even in the context of the Faith Chapter of the Bible—Hebrews 11—we find once again that faith depends on evidence:

- By faith the people passed through the Red Sea as on dry land; but when the Egyptians tried to do so, they were drowned (Hebrews 11:29).

The Israelites could not be certain that the piled-up waters of the Red Sea would not engulf them as they passed through. Yet they trusted in God's instructions and that is exactly what they did, making their way forward with walls of sea water on both sides of them.

While the Israelites were still in Egypt, they had witnessed the ten plagues that had devastated the land. At the same time, they had experienced God Almighty's divine protection—no harm had come to them! They had absolute proof that the same God who had led them out of Egypt would perform an incredible miracle for them at the Red Sea.

From these examples, we can see that the faith of the Israelites was not an evidence-less, blind faith. On the contrary, theirs was a faith that had a strong evidential foundation. God had proved Himself to them.

While it is true that the Bible commands us to have faith, never once does it command us to have faith in the absence of evidence.

Repeatedly, Moses admonished the Israelites to have faith because of what they had already seen God miraculously do for them:

- "If you say in your heart, 'These nations are greater than I. How can I dispossess them?' you shall not be afraid of them but you shall remember what the LORD your God did to Pharaoh and to all Egypt, the great trials that your eyes saw, the signs, the wonders, the mighty hand, and the outstretched arm, by which the LORD your God brought you out. So will the LORD your God do to all the peoples of whom you are afraid" (Deuteronomy 7:17-19).

Moses reminded Israel that they already had a sufficient evidential basis for their faith. The Israelites just needed to remember the miracles that God had done on their behalf. In light of this, a failure to walk in faith did not represent a lack of evidence but rather a failure to rationally consider the evidence already available.

After two miraculous feedings of many thousands, Jesus' disciples worried that they didn't have enough bread. At this point, they should have known that Jesus was more than able to supply any lack of food, and so Jesus castigated them:

- "O you of little faith, why are you discussing among yourselves the fact that you have no bread? Do you not yet perceive? Do you not remember the five loaves for the five thousand, and how many baskets you gathered? Or the seven loaves for the four thousand, and how many baskets you gathered? How is it that you fail to understand that I did not speak about bread? Beware of the leaven of the Pharisees and Sadducees" (Matthew 16:8-11).

Jesus wasn't asking His disciples to make a blind leap of faith. He merely wanted them to remember how He had provided for them on other occasions.

In fact, Jesus never wanted blind faith from His disciples, back then or even now. I am sure that what He would like to see in His followers is the full exercise of their God-given minds.

This brings us back to Richard Dawkins' comments at the beginning of the chapter, where he insists that biblical faith is a rejection of the mind. Actually, biblical faith is the very opposite—it is, in fact, the rejection of mindlessness.

Works Cited

"Richard Dawkins." BrainyQuote.com. Xplore Inc, January 2016, www.brainyquote.com/quotes/quotes/r/richarddaw 141335.html. Accessed 7 September 2016.

Chapter 6

THE HOLY SPIRIT: ARE SCRIPTURE AND THEOLOGY IRRELEVANT?

CHAPTER SUMMARY
The Spirit works in conjunction with the Word and not apart from it. Those who claim to be led by the Spirit apart from the Word, like some Quaker sects, must find confirmation for their intuitions elsewhere.

Today, the idea of comprehensively studying the Word is being undermined in a number of different ways.

In one branch of Quakerism, there is no sermon or Scripture. Instead, all sit quietly until "the Spirit" stirs someone to get up and speak. Writing in the first half of the twentieth century, one of their guiding lights, Rufus Jones, wrote that the Quaker...

- "...turns away from arid theological notions and insists instead upon a real and vital experience of God revealed to persons in their own souls" (Jones).

From what Jones says, we can deduce that some Quakers find scriptural teachings and doctrine dry and lifeless. Although Jones insists on turning away from "arid theological notions," his claim is highly theological and perhaps "arid," as well.

Nevertheless, Jones is right that God can speak to us in many ways, even directly into our heart and mind, as Scripture clearly asserts:

- For even though they knew God [through their minds, senses, emotions, and the creation], they did not honor him as God or give thanks, but they became futile in their speculations, and their foolish heart was darkened (Romans 1:21).

- "And He, when He comes, will convict the world concerning sin and righteousness and judgment" (John 16:8).

In fact, the wisdom of God is all around us, crying out to be taken by all:

- Out in the open wisdom calls aloud, she raises her voice in the public square; on top of the wall she cries out, at the city gate she makes her speech: "How long will you who are simple love your simple ways? How long will mockers delight in mockery and fools hate knowledge? Repent at my rebuke! Then I will pour out my thoughts to you, I will make known to you my teachings. But since you refuse to listen when I call and no one pays attention when I stretch out my hand…" (Proverbs 1:20-24)

So, we can see that wisdom is readily available, and yet it is rejected. Why is this?

The path of wisdom is painful. It carries with it a personal rebuke. After all, the first step towards wisdom requires us to see the truth about ourselves and repent. Of course, this is the last thing in the world we want to do. It is only after we confront our own blindness—through confession and repentance—that we can see clearly enough to correct others (Matthew 7:1-5).

However, according to the words of Jesus in a passage we have looked at before, we prefer to hide away in the darkness of our denial and rationalizations:

- "This is the verdict: Light has come into the world, but people loved darkness instead of light because their deeds were evil. Everyone who does evil hates the light, and will not come into the light for fear that their deeds will be exposed" (John 3:19-20).

Consequently, unless we are being drawn into the light of truth, we will grow to hate it. In order to cover up this hatred, we might even boast that we are seeking the light. We might even declare that the Holy Spirit is leading us.

It is easy for us to avoid the light and congratulate ourselves by believing that our feelings and personal sentiments are those of the Spirit. And, if we are convinced that this is so, then the "Spirit" would *never* tell us anything that would contradict our agenda. How convenient!

Instead, Scripture warns us of our almost limitless ability to delude ourselves concerning matters of the Spirit:

- All a man's ways seem right to him, but the LORD weighs the heart (Proverbs 21:2).

- Thus says the LORD of hosts, "Do not listen to the words of the prophets who are prophesying to you. They are leading you into futility; *they speak a vision of their own imagination*, not from the mouth of the LORD" (Jeremiah 23:16, emphasis added).

- Then the LORD said to me, "The prophets are prophesying falsehood in my name. I have neither sent them nor commanded them nor spoken to them; they are prophesying to you a false vision, divination, futility *and the deception of their own minds*" (Jeremiah 14:14, emphasis added).

- Thus says the Lord GOD, "Woe to the foolish prophets *who are following their own spirit* and have seen nothing" (Ezekiel 13:3, emphasis added).

How is it that we can be so horribly deceived?

There are two reasons for this—one voluntary and one involuntary. We voluntarily harden ourselves to God. According to the truth found in Romans 1:18-32, we harden our hearts and become defenseless before the darkness of self-delusion.

Other verses corroborate this idea:

- "But my people would not listen to me; Israel would not submit to me. So I gave them over to their stubborn hearts to follow their own devices" (Psalm 81:11-12; 2 Peter 2:18-21).

We must also contend with immaturity. Growth into the light takes time, as Jesus indicated:

- "If you hold to my teaching, you are really my disciples. *Then* you will know the truth, and the truth *will* set you free" (John 8:31-32, emphasis added).

It's a process!

Sound theology does not just suddenly appear in our lives, fully formed and appreciated. The Holy Spirit gives us wisdom, over the course of time, through our study of the Word:

- Oh, how I love your law! I meditate on it all day long. Your commands make me wiser than my enemies, for they are ever with me. I have more insight than all my teachers, for I meditate on your statutes. I have more understanding than the elders, for I obey your precepts (Psalm 119:97-100).

Meditation on the Scriptures is most definitely a process. It requires time but, in conjunction with the illumination of the Holy Spirit, it does indeed produce wisdom:

- The law of the LORD is perfect, reviving the soul. The statutes of the LORD are trustworthy, *making wise the simple* (Psalm 19:7, emphasis added).

In addition, let us not forget that the Spirit can also use the wisdom that comes from Scripture to lead us to salvation. This was Timothy's experience:

- How from infancy you have known the holy Scriptures, which are able to make you wise for salvation through faith in Christ Jesus (2 Timothy 3:15).

* * * * *

Let us now return to some of the claims of Rufus Jones and the Quakers.

Does the Holy Spirit work apart from Scripture, as Jones claims? He certainly can, but instead, He has ordained that His normative work takes place through Scripture.

Here is how Paul explains it:

- How, then, can they call on the one they have not believed in? And how can they believe in the one of whom they have not heard? And how can they hear without someone preaching to them? And how can they preach unless they are sent? As it is written, "How beautiful are the feet of those who bring good news!"...Consequently, faith comes from hearing the message, and the message is heard through the word of Christ (Romans 10:14-15, 17).

When we examine what Jones said, it is obvious that his faith was not based on hearing the message of the Gospel. Since that was the case, then perhaps it would have been wise for him to question the efficacy of his faith, as Isaiah counseled long ago...

- When men tell you to consult mediums and spiritists, who whisper and mutter, should not a people inquire of their God? Why consult the dead on behalf of the living? To the law and to the testimony! If they do not speak according to this word, they have no light of dawn (Isaiah 8:19-20).

Paul taught clearly that, when we go beyond Scripture, we go beyond the wisdom of God. And that can get us into trouble. We would do well to remember Paul's words in I Corinthians 4:6: "Do not go beyond what is written."

If we want to be faithful to our Lord, we must be faithful to His Word:

- If anyone speaks, he should do it as one speaking the very words of God (1 Peter 4:11).

When Paul departed from the Ephesian elders for the last time, he pronounced this benediction upon them:

- "Now I commit you to God and to the word of his grace, which can build you up and give you an inheritance among all those who are sanctified" (Acts 20:32).

According to Peter, blessing comes through the Word, *not the Spirit alone*:

- His divine power has given us everything we need for life and godliness through our knowledge of him who called us by his own glory and goodness. *Through these he has given us his very great and precious promises*, so that through them you may participate in the divine nature and escape the corruption in the world caused by evil desires (2 Peter 1:3-4, emphasis added).

As we continue to consider the importance of the Word, let us ask another very pertinent question: What does it mean to be a follower of Christ? Jesus answers this in many ways. He warned:

- "If anyone does not remain in me, he is like a branch that is thrown away and withers; such branches are picked up, thrown into the fire and burned" (John 15:6).

Well then, the next question for us to consider is this: What does it mean to remain in Him?

Here is Jesus' explanation:

- "If you remain in me and my words remain in you, ask whatever you wish, and it will be given you…If you obey my commands, you will remain in my love, just as I have obeyed my Father's commands and remain in his love…You are my friends if you do what I command" (John 15:7, 10,14).

Abiding in the Spirit alone is not enough. There is no other way to be a friend of God except to abide faithfully in His Word.

We need to remember that the Spirit is the author of Scripture. He led its writers to write what they did (1 Peter 1:9-10; 2 Peter 1:19-21). It is therefore impossible to abide in the Spirit without also abiding in His Word. And without the Spirit, understanding and discerning the Word of God is not possible:

- The person without the Spirit does not accept the things that come from the Spirit of God but considers them foolishness, and cannot understand them because they are discerned only through the Spirit (1 Corinthians 2:14).

In the Gospels, Jesus also taught about the inseparable nature of Word and Spirit:

- "The Spirit gives life; the flesh counts for nothing. *The words I have spoken to you are Spirit and they are life*" (John 6:63, emphasis added).

Because they are so connected, we cannot claim that we have the Spirit if we reject the Word. If we are not born of the Spirit through the Word, we can have little assurance that we are being led by the Spirit.

Contrary to what Rufus Jones might say, the teachings of Christ were far from being "arid theological notions." Our Lord taught living and essential truths, as He always claimed:

- "I have come into the world as a light, so that no one who believes in me should stay in darkness...For I did not speak of my own accord, but the Father who sent me commanded me what to say and how to say it. I know that *his command leads to eternal life*..." (John 12:46, 49-50, emphasis added).

Not just the Quakers, but many others claim scriptural support for the notion that, since they are being led by the Spirit, they do not need the Word of the Spirit. For textual "back-up," they cite these verses:

- But you have an anointing from the Holy One, and all of you know the truth...As for you, the anointing you received from him remains in you, and you do not need anyone to teach you. But as his anointing teaches you about all things and as that anointing is real, not counterfeit—just as it has taught you, remain in him (1 John 2:20, 27).

To conclude that the Word is not necessary when one is led by the Spirit is clearly mistaken, as we have shown in previous paragraphs. Yet, another reason for the error in this kind of thinking can be found as we examine this passage from I John. For, if Scripture had been made unnecessary by the work of the Spirit, then surely there would be no need for teachers of Scripture. But this is clearly not true:

- It was he [God] who gave some to be apostles, some to be prophets, some to be evangelists, and some to be pastors and teachers, to prepare God's people for works of service, so that the body of Christ may be built up until we all reach unity in the faith and in the knowledge of the Son of God and become mature, attaining to the whole measure of the fullness of Christ (Ephesians 4:11-13).

So then, what happens when we don't elevate the Word to its proper place? The effect is profound. Without the Word, we don't have a proper foundation for our faith and are blown about by every wind of doctrine.

For decades, I had struggled unsuccessfully against depression. Even after coming to the Lord, I was consumed by powerful feelings that God did not like me and might not have accepted me. It was so natural for me to assume that these powerful feelings were the leading of the Spirit. However, Scripture trumped these feelings and convinced me that they did not accurately represent the Spirit's true view of me.

* * * * *

There are many who claim to have the guidance of the Spirit, and yet some things about their lives just don't make sense.

One pastor claimed that the Spirit had led him to divorce his wife and marry a younger woman. The congregation agreed, believing that these personal leadings took precedence over Scripture. However, some years later, this same pastor received another "revelation" from the Spirit to divorce his second wife in favor of a much younger woman. It was only then that his congregation began to ask questions.

There are many people, like this pastor, who claim that they are led by the Spirit to commit sin. How are conundrums like this to be addressed? There must be a source higher than our personal feelings, a foundation more dependable than the way we "sense" the Spirit is guiding us.

That reliable source is Scripture.

How then do we interpret 1 John 2:20 and 27? Let's take another look:

- But you have an anointing from the Holy One, and all of you know the truth…As for you, the anointing you received from him remains in you, and you do not need anyone to teach you. But as his anointing teaches you about all things and as that anointing is real, not counterfeit—just as it has taught you, remain in him (1 John 2:20, 27).

These verses *never* say that the Spirit teaches us *apart* from Scripture. Instead, His anointing teaches us *through* Scripture, including the teachings of the Apostles.

John wrote about these things in the first chapter of this same letter:

- We proclaim to you what we have seen and heard, so that you also may have fellowship with us. And our fellowship is with the Father and with his Son, Jesus

Christ. We write this to make our joy complete (1 John 1:3-4).

It all starts with the proclaimed Gospel. And consider this: if the Spirit's anointing was all that was required, John would have had absolutely no reason to write this letter!

Here is how he concludes his epistle:

- We know also that the Son of God has come and has given us *understanding* [through His teachings], so that we may know him who is true. And we are in him who is true—even in his Son Jesus Christ. He is the true God and eternal life (1 John 5:20, emphasis added).

According to John, salvation came through the teachings of Jesus...*not apart from the anointing of the Spirit, but in conjunction with it!*

Works Cited

Jones, Rufus. "An Interpretation of Quakerism." Philadelphia Yearly Meeting of the Religious Society of Friends, 1981, www.pym.org/publications/pym-pamphlets/an-interpretation-of-quakerism/. Accessed October 2015.

PART II

Chapter 7

THE ESSENTIAL NATURE OF THEOLOGY

CHAPTER SUMMARY

Jesus was a champion of systematic theology. If we fail to understand the Bible thoroughly and comprehensively, rightly dividing the Word of truth, we will fail to harvest the riches that come with an assured understanding.

Many Christians wrongly claim:

I don't need theology. I just believe what the Bible says!

Theology has become a dirty word, along with "doctrine" and "dogma." But it is, in fact, indispensable. How else can we know what the Bible teaches?

If we take Psalm 1 and Joshua 1:8 seriously, and meditate on the Word day and night, serious work is required. We cannot simply take one verse in isolation from the rest of Scripture. All of the verses of the Bible are a unity. Diligent theological work is essential in order to rightly relate each verse to the context of the rest of Scripture.

Let's do some of this "work" as we study Jesus' ministry of healing on the Sabbath.

The enemies of Jesus claimed that He was sinning because, when He healed a man, He was violating the command against working on the Sabbath (Deuteronomy 5:12-15).

However, Jesus responded that His accusers were not judging biblically, but superficially:

- "Now if a boy can be circumcised on the Sabbath so that the law of Moses may not be broken, why are you angry with me for healing a man's whole body on the Sabbath? Stop judging by mere appearances, but instead judge correctly" (John 7:23-24).

In the same way, we cannot judge simply from the "appearance" of a single verse. Instead, we have to understand how that verse fits, not only into its immediate context, *but also into the entire context of all of God's teachings.* In other words, in order to properly understand a single verse, we have to understand that verse in conjunction with all of the verses on the subject.

This is the very thing that Jesus' detractors were not doing. Therefore, Jesus tried to instruct them with a more comprehensive exposition of the subject.

On one occasion, He argued that the keeping of the Sabbath had to be understood in light of its many exceptions. With a grand display of comprehensive, systematic theology, Jesus cited the fact that David had broken the Sabbath and had picked grain from the fields to feed his hungry men. He reminded them that the priests also worked on the Sabbath. And finally—perhaps to indicate His divinity—Jesus concluded by declaring Himself to be the Lord of the Sabbath! (Matthew 12:8)

On another occasion, Jesus healed a woman in the synagogue. To the great consternation of the leadership, Jesus astutely reminded them that they too worked on the Sabbath by caring for their animals on that day. Therefore, they were being hypocritical for criticizing Him for healing the woman, who was more valuable than their animals (Luke 13).

In all these instances, Jesus had provided badly needed lessons on the work of theology, comparing Scripture with Scripture.

The temple leadership had also been doing theology, but their use of it failed to appreciate and consider the entire body of Scripture. Instead, they were merely emphasizing one verse among the many verses dealing with the Sabbath.

We all do theology. But some of us aren't aware of it and, therefore, perform it in a haphazard rather than in a systematic and comprehensive way.

Let's look at an example of doing theology that goes to the heart of the Gospel.

In Psalm 7, David called upon God to judge him according to *his* righteousness:

- The Lord shall judge the people: judge me, O Lord, *according to my righteousness*, and *according to mine integrity that is in me* (Psalm 7:8, KJV, emphasis added).

This sounds arrogant. How can any of us stand before God in our own righteousness? If we were to ask God for justice—for what we deserve—He would condemn the lot of us:

- Now we know that whatever the law says it speaks to those who are under the law, so that every mouth may be stopped, and the whole world may be held accountable to God. For by works of the law no human being will be justified in his sight, since through the law comes knowledge of sin...for all have sinned and fall short of the glory of God...(Romans 3:19-20, 23)

There are many verses that deny that we deserve *anything* good from God by virtue of our own righteousness or integrity.

And all of these verses would apparently line themselves up contrary to David's hope. Both Paul and James had insisted that just one sin would condemn us to death. Only the free gift of God is able to provide us with any basis for hope (Romans 6:23; James 2:10).

If anyone rejects theology, he is faced with this paradox—that, on the one hand, our hope is in our own righteousness, as David prayed. And yet, from what Paul, James and others say, we should have no hope at all in any so-called righteousness of our own.

Believing both of these truths at face value is a sure prescription for confusion and uncertainty. Therefore, the dilemma must be resolved through serious study.

Interestingly, David himself also acknowledged that we are sinners who require the mercy of God:

- Blessed is the one whose transgression is forgiven, whose sin is covered. Blessed is the man against whom the LORD counts no iniquity, and in whose spirit there is no deceit. For when I kept silent, my bones wasted away through my groaning all day long. For day and night your hand was heavy upon me; my strength was dried up as by the heat of summer. I acknowledged my sin to you, and I did not cover my iniquity; I said, "I will confess my transgressions to the LORD," and you forgave the iniquity of my sin (Psalm 32:1-5).

Well then, if David understood that his blessedness derived from God's forgiveness and not his own merit, how could he be so brash as to ask God to judge him *according to his own righteousness?*

A little systematic theology can reconcile these two truths.

In Psalm 7, David had been standing upon his righteousness in terms of his innocence regarding a *specific* wrongdoing:

- O LORD my God, if I have done this, if there is wrong in my hands, if I have repaid my friend with evil or plundered my enemy without cause…(Psalm 7:3-4)

David wasn't claiming a total righteous standing before God, but rather his innocence in regards to his enemy. He was asking for justice in this particular criminal matter alone.

Therefore, David pleaded:

- Oh, let the evil of the wicked come to an end, and may you establish the righteous—you who test the minds and hearts, O righteous God! (Psalm 7:9)

There are two different aspects of justice. Before God, we are *all* guilty. However, before man, there are important distinctions between the innocent and the guilty. David knew he wasn't righteous before God. However, in regards to his enemies, he knew he was innocent.

Unless our theology includes a comprehensive study of Scripture, we cannot rightly interpret the Word of truth. And this is something we are required to do:

- Do your best to present yourself to God as one approved, a worker who has no need to be ashamed, rightly handling the word of truth (2 Timothy 2:15).

Fundamentally, it is God who requires us to be serious students of the Bible. Why is this? Unless we are comprehensive— including in our studies the Hebrew Scriptures and all the gospels and epistles of the New Testament—we may end up with erroneous and seemingly contradictory conclusions.

Let's take, for another example, these two troubling verses:

- Whosoever abideth in him sinneth not: whosoever sinneth hath not seen him, neither known him…Whosoever is born of God doth not commit sin; for his seed remaineth in him: and he cannot sin, because he is born of God (1 John 3:6, 9, KJV).

These verses are troubling for a number of reasons. For one thing, they seem to contradict other verses, even what John had written earlier:

- If we say that we have no sin, we deceive ourselves, and the truth is not in us. If we confess our sins, he is faithful and just to forgive us our sins, and to cleanse us from all unrighteousness. If we say that we have not sinned, we make him a liar, and his word is not in us (1 John 1:8-10, KJV).

While 1 John 3 claims that the saved *do not sin*, 1 John 1 claims that the saved *do sin*—a direct contradiction!

In addition, the doubts and inner turmoil caused by 1 John 3:9 are just as problematic as the "contradiction." How can any of us be confident that we are saved after we read, "Whosoever is born of God doth not commit [any] sin"?

None of us can say this! Such a perspective calls into question our understanding of the message of the Good News. If only the morally perfect can be saved, then the Good News is not Good News for anyone.

However, there is an easy resolution to this problem.

The KJV phrase, "sinneth not," can also be understood to mean "…does not continue in the practice of sin." This is the interpretation of the modern translations:

- No one who abides in him *keeps on sinning*; no one who *keeps on sinning* has either seen him or known him...No one born of God *makes a practice of sinning*, for God's seed abides in him, and *he cannot keep on sinning because he has been born of God* (1 John 3:6, 9, ESV, emphasis added).

According to these modern renderings, it is not a matter of a Christian not sinning at all, but whether a Christian is sinning as the product of an unrepentant lifestyle. In light of updated translations, this problems evaporates. The Good News remains Good News, and any contradiction is resolved.

Doing theology—serious study of the Bible in order to understand it as a unified revelation—is necessary so that we can understand God and His ways. According to Paul, the result of this hard work is riches. He therefore prayed:

- That their hearts may be encouraged, being knit together in love, to reach all the riches of full assurance of understanding and the knowledge of God's mystery, which is Christ, in whom are hidden all the treasures of wisdom and knowledge. I say this in order that no one may delude you with plausible arguments (Colossians 2:2-4).

These "riches" consist of the "full assurance of understanding." However, such treasures of understanding are not possible unless we meditate on the Word day and night. That is the way we can truly derive the Word's meaning.

Paul reasoned that if we come to acquire these "treasures of wisdom and knowledge," we will not be deluded or carried away by arguments and the temptations of other treasures, which we fear we might be lacking.

Instead, Scripture teaches us that we have riches beyond calculation:

- See to it that no one takes you captive by philosophy and empty deceit, according to human tradition, according to the elemental spirits of the world, and not according to Christ. For in him the whole fullness of deity dwells bodily, and you have been filled in him, who is the head of all rule and authority (Colossians 2:8-10).

If we truly grasp the extent of our blessedness, we will not be lured away.

Chapter 8

THEOLOGICAL CONTEMPLATION

CHAPTER SUMMARY
Confidence and a robust Christian life requires that we resolve apparent contradictions, recognizing the manipulation of Scripture so that we are not deceived. We must also judge ourselves by the light of Scripture—but of course we must first understand it.

Our confidence about Scripture largely depends upon our understanding of it. If we are confused because its teachings seem to be contradictory, it will be difficult for us to live a robust and faith-filled Christian life. Why is this? The answer is simple—because it is hard to believe in something if it doesn't make any sense!

Instead, if we are to live a vibrant and confident Christian life, we must know that we are standing upon solid ground. This requires serious theological contemplation of the Word:

- But his delight is in the law of the Lord, and on his law he meditates day and night. He is like a tree planted by streams of water that yields its fruit in its season, and its leaf does not wither. In all that he does, he prospers (Psalm 1:2-3).

Our God wants to be known and worshiped for who He is (John 4:23-24). Therefore, He rewards our diligence in His Word, which is a treasure-trove of His knowledge.

However, there are times when we meditate on the Word and we are faced with an apparent contradiction that needs to be resolved. (Of course, it is impossible for us to resolve each of the Scriptural dilemmas that we face. Some are irresolvable, at least for now. I will deal with this in the next chapter.)

Some of these challenges are being thrust upon us by our post-Christian society. For example, in his zeal to flaunt what he considers to be the Bible's "contradictions," New Testament critic Bart Ehrman claims that the Pastoral Epistles are forgeries. Furthermore, he claims that the Pastorals present a different means of salvation than Paul's other Epistles:

- For Paul himself, only through the death and resurrection of Jesus can a person be saved. And for the Pastorals? For women, at least, we're told in 1 Timothy 2 that they will be saved by bearing children (Ehrman 100).

To support what he thinks is a contradiction, Ehrman cites this particular verse from Paul's first letter to Timothy:

- Yet she will be saved through childbearing—if they continue in faith and love and holiness, with self-control (1 Timothy 2:15).

Well, this certainly seems to be a contradiction, right? (When we talk about this in class, I chide my single female students that I know a good matchmaker so that they can begin to bear children and thus be saved!)

However—all kidding aside—this verse confuses women and, I suspect, also troubles them. After all, this idea seems to directly contradict other verses that teach us that salvation is a free gift, like Ephesians 2:8-9.

However, there is a way out of this difficulty. You see, Bart Ehrman has conveniently failed to tell us that the word "saved" can be used in at least two different ways:

1. Saved from eternal damnation, or…
2. …saved from physical death!

The verse that Ehrman cites as proof of a contradiction actually means this: a woman bearing a child will be saved from the threat of physical death in the midst of the ordeal of childbearing. This use of the word has nothing to do with damnation.

How do we know this? By doing serious Bible study—theology! We carefully examine the context and find that it relates back to the Fall and God's curse upon the woman:

- For Adam was formed first, then Eve; and Adam was not deceived, but the woman was deceived and became a transgressor [Genesis 3]. Yet she will be saved through childbearing—if they continue in faith and love and holiness, with self-control (1 Timothy 2:13-15).

Clearly, the woman's life will be *physically* "saved" through the painful ordeal of childbearing. This verse has nothing to do with eternal salvation.

But how can we be sure that Paul is using the second definition of the word "saved," the definition that refers to physical death? Once again, diligent study of the context—theology—takes us back to Eve's original sin and the curse of "pain in childbearing":

- To the woman he [God] said, "I will surely multiply your pain in childbearing; in pain you shall bring forth children" (Genesis 3:16).

In light of this, 1 Timothy promises that the woman "will be saved [from the danger of physical death because of the "curse"] through [the ordeal of] childbearing." Contradiction resolved!

If we fail to reconcile apparent contradictions in the Scriptures, they will whittle away at our confidence in Christ, our clarity of mind, and our willingness to be a light. All of these will be in jeopardy.

For example, if a woman has not had a child, this verse might destroy her confidence that she indeed belongs to Christ. This uncertainty might give rise to doubts about her salvation. She might even find herself wondering whether the Christian faith makes any sense at all.

Unless issues like this are resolved, moving forward confidently in our faith becomes increasingly difficult. If we cannot answer these kinds of questions when we are faced with them, we might withdraw from situations that could be confrontational. Our zeal for evangelism would dry up.

A recent Pew survey revealed that atheists know more about the Christian faith than Christians! Should it be any surprise, then, that atheists are driving us out of the public marketplace of ideas? As a consequence, those who are biblical skeptics have managed to gain control of all of the centers of influence in our country.

To offer up just one example of the amazing reach of these skeptics, it is clear that the narrative about homosexuality is controlled by the media, Hollywood, and the universities. In fact, in many places, these cultural "institutions" are even in control of the biblical narrative on homosexuality.

Here is an example of what I mean…

In *The Good Book*, the late Harvard seminary professor, Peter Gomes, argued that Jesus "was under the impression that Sodom was destroyed because it lacked hospitality" (Gomes Ch. 8). In defense of this bizarre position, he cited Ezekiel:

- "'Behold, this was the guilt of your sister Sodom: she and her daughters had pride, excess of food, and prosperous ease, but did not aid the poor and needy'" (Ezekiel 16:49).

This seems to support Gomes' case until we proceed on to the next verse:

- "'They were haughty and did an *abomination* before me. So I removed them, when I saw it'" (Ezekiel 16:50, emphasis added).

The Hebrew word for "abomination"—*toebah*—is also used to condemn homosexuality:

- "You shall not lie with a male as with a woman; it is an abomination" (Leviticus 18:22; 20:13).

Gomes also neglected to mention what Jude wrote:

- And the angels who did not stay within their own position of authority, but left their proper dwelling, he has kept in eternal chains under gloomy darkness until the judgment of the great day—just as Sodom and Gomorrah and the surrounding cities, which likewise indulged in *sexual immorality and pursued unnatural desire*, serve as an example by undergoing a punishment of eternal fire (Jude 1:6-7, emphasis added).

There is a lesson to be learned here. If we fail to diligently study the Bible, we will be easily led astray, with vast consequences for the surrounding culture.

* * * * *

Perhaps the place where we must stay most theologically alert is within the Church. This is where we tend to let down our theological guard.

Popular "Prosperity Gospel" speaker, Joyce Meyer, abuses Scripture, as do many in the so-called "name-it-claim-it" movement:

- Meyer also believes that people can speak things into existence: "It says in Romans 4:17 that…we have a God who gives life to the dead and He calls things that be not as though they already existed…If there's something in your way, speak to it…" (Hunter)

Does Romans 4 actually suggest that we have the power to speak things into existence the way that God does?

- As it is written, "I have made you the father of many nations"—in the presence of the God in whom he believed, who gives life to the dead and calls into existence the things that do not exist (Romans 4:17).

There is nothing in Scripture—either in this verse or anywhere else—that suggests we have such power.

Meyer also proposes that if we have sown seeds in a positive "account" in heaven, we can draw from it as we wish:

- "When I talked with Dr. Roberts today and we talked about this seed-faith thing, he said…when you give you get a receipt in heaven that when you have a need you can then go with your receipt and say, 'You see, God, I have got my receipt from my sowing and now I have a need and I'm cashing in my receipt'" (Hunter).

However, Meyer is overlooking the fact that no one has a positive account. Instead of thinking that we are worthy enough to draw what we deserve from heaven, Jesus counseled us to regard ourselves as unworthy:

- "So you also, when you have done all that you were commanded, say, 'We are unworthy servants; we have only done what was our duty'" (Luke 17:10).

Therefore, according to the words of Jesus, even the most obedient among us must regard ourselves as unworthy! The only hope that any of us have is in the mercy of God, who is never in a position to owe us anything:

- "Who has ever given to God, that God should repay him?" (Romans 11:35)

The "Prosperity Gospel" is an offense before God.

How then can we avoid being offensive? By understanding and abiding in His Word:

- "If you abide in me, and my words abide in you, ask whatever you wish, and it will be done for you. By this my Father is glorified…If you keep my commandments, you will abide in my love, just as I have kept my Father's commandments and abide in his love. These things I have spoken to you, that my joy may be in you, and that your joy may be full" (John 15:7-11).

I am still trying to weed out of my life the ideas that are offensive to God. And, I freely admit that when I came to God, I was overflowing with repugnant ideas.

Having experienced considerable anti-Semitism, I hated "Whites" and was actually convinced that they had a nauseating odor. Even after the Lord had revealed Himself to me, the idea of entering a church was traumatic. When I started to attend, I was convinced that all the white people in the pews around me were hypocrites.

Scripture and Christian maturity required that I scrutinize my every thought by His Word. I knew that I had to do this—a long and painful process. Eventually, as I studied the Scriptures, good fruit began to grow where once there had only been weeds.

Works Cited

Ehrman, Bart. *Forged: Writing in the Name of God—Why the Bible's Authors Are Not Who We Think They Are.* HarperCollins, 2012.

Gomes, Peter J. *The Good Book: Reading the Bible with Mind and Heart.* HarperSanFrancisco, 1996.

Hunter, Bob. "Christianity Still in Crisis?" *Christian Research Journal,* vol. 30, no. 3, 2007.

Chapter 9

THE MYSTERIES
OF THE FAITH

CHAPTER SUMMARY
Although we must try to understand Scripture in a harmonious way, we can also overdo it. We often negate what Scripture is saying so that we can fit everything into our limited worldview. Finally, how do we resolve the age-old issue of our responsibilities vs. God's sovereignty?

While we seek understanding from the Scriptures, we need to face this reality: we will never understand everything.

The Trinity is the prime example of this—that God is One but also Three.

Another pertinent example is this—that we take responsibility for our lives and make freewill choices even though God has the primary responsibility.

Before I begin to deal with this issue, I would first of all like to point out that the Christian life must be a proactive life. Here is how Paul represented our lives in Christ:

- Do you not know that in a race all the runners run, but only one receives the prize? So run that you may obtain it. Every athlete exercises self-control in all things. They do it to receive a perishable wreath, but we an imperishable. So I do not run aimlessly; I do not box as one beating the air. But I discipline my body and keep it under control, lest after preaching to others I myself should be disqualified (1 Corinthians 9:24-27).

It is a truth we cannot deny—the Christian life is strenuous; there is nothing passive about it.

Now, let me give you a personal example. I am a highly irritable and anxious person. This means that there are a lot of things that set me off. Ugh! Even my beloved wife, from time to time, steps on my elongated toes—my exaggerated sensitivities.

If I am in a potentially anxious situation and do not respond proactively, I inevitably begin to brood. In my mind, I will naturally gravitate to the worst thoughts and outcomes. But over the years I have learned—for the sake of my marriage— that I must contend strenuously against my natural defaults.

Here is what I do:

1. I pray and forgive;
2. I confess my wrong response and try to understand what triggered it;
3. I lavish my wife with words of love and appreciation;
4. I proactively go the extra mile and perform an act of love to turn the situation into a victory!

Sounds like a good plan, right?

However, are we not counseled to wait on the Lord, as Isaiah 40:31 prescribes? The answer to that question is, "Not literally." Instead, the "waiting" involved in stressful circumstances is understanding and acknowledging in our hearts that deliverance comes from the Lord.

And yet, there is a part for us to play—we must act. We need to realize that God often rescues us through our efforts. And these efforts are actually part of His provision for us.

Let's take a look at the way Paul presented this wonderful truth:

- But by the grace of God I am what I am, and his grace toward me was not in vain. On the contrary, I worked harder than any of them, though it was not I, but the grace of God that is with me (1 Corinthians 15:10).

In this verse, Paul is confessing that even his efforts came from God.

But—you might be thinking—how can it be both? How can God's provision and our efforts coexist harmoniously in our lives?

I do not think that we can understand it completely, but this paradox is clearly infused throughout the biblical revelation. Even though we are entirely responsible for our lives, God is even more so:

- For we are God's workmanship, created in Christ Jesus to do good works, which God prepared in advance for us to do (Ephesians 2:10).

In other words, if we are to embrace the entirety of revelation, we need to accept the fact that we indeed are to run the race to win the crown of life...*that our Lord has already bequeathed us!*

Does this make sense? Not completely. But how can we expect to totally understand everything our Heavenly Father reveals to us? That is why we need to continue to seek understanding and, at the same time, live proactively.

* * * * *

As we contemplate some of the great mysteries of our faith, we also need to be careful. It is a very dangerous thing to force difficult biblical teachings to agree with one another when they really don't—at least as far as our finite human understanding is concerned.

For example, returning to an issue I mentioned at the beginning of this chapter, how can we coerce teachings on the Trinity to agree? The Church has a long and sad history of trying to do this very thing. To force these teachings into a theology that we can humanly grasp, the Church has either denied the humanity of Christ—Docetism—or the divinity of Christ—Arianism.

By impelling Scripture to take one side or the other—Christ's humanity or His deity—we have violated God's revelation to us. And we miss something in that process. We wrongly assume that we should be able to systematize everything in Scripture in order to conform all the data to our limited understanding.

However, even scientists recognize that they cannot do this— despite having all the data of research and science at their disposal. They have learned that they cannot coerce all of the findings of science into the confines of their narrow human theories. Instead, they have come to understand that they need to allow the data to speak for itself.

Let's look at just one germane area of scientific study to illustrate this point.

Sub-atomic physics does not agree with Newtonian physics. Scientists who study in these areas can either ignore certain findings that do not agree with their theories, or they can allow the paradoxical elements to force them to dig more deeply.

Theologians must do the same thing. They must not dismiss or change the Scriptural data that does not fit into their conception of the God-Head. Instead, they must accept all the data—all the appropriate verses—however perplexing they might be.

Let's examine another contentious area of biblical study—the divide between Arminianism and Calvinism.

We cannot dismiss or modify those verses that picture God's absolute sovereignty as some—the Arminians—do. But neither can we dismiss or degrade human responsibility as others—the Calvinists—are tempted to do. Somehow, both of these sets of Scriptural teachings must be embraced. Although we do not completely understand how, these seemingly oppositional perspectives are compatible.

Sometimes, a single verse contains both perspectives, as if to say, "There is absolutely no disagreement between God's sovereign control over our lives and our responsibility to strenuously pursue the things of God." Here is one of those verses, which we considered earlier in this chapter:

- But by the grace of God I am what I am, and his grace toward me was not in vain. On the contrary, I worked harder than any of them, though it was not I, but the grace of God that is with me (1 Corinthians 15:10).

Strangely, Paul credited God for all the good that came out of his life, even his hard work! He never said, "Because I am what I am by the grace of God, I am going to settle back and just wait for Him to do all the heavy lifting." Although God is sovereign, reigning over our lives and directing our steps, it certainly does not mean that we abdicate our responsibilities.

How do we understand this?

Yet again, we are faced with what seems to be a contradiction. If, according to Ephesians 2:10, we are His workmanship, then shouldn't we be letting Him do the work?

No! God achieves His purposes through our freewill efforts.

But does this fully explain our relationship with our Savior? Not completely.

However, if we are to be faithful to Scripture, we must embrace both perspectives, even though we do not completely understand how they fit together.

Here is another example—two sets of verses that seem to be in contradiction:

- For I am sure that neither death nor life, nor angels, nor rulers, nor things present, nor things to come, nor powers, nor height, nor depth, nor anything else in all creation, will be able to separate us from the love of God in Christ Jesus our Lord (Romans 8:38-39).

- But I discipline my body and keep it under control, lest after preaching to others, I myself should be disqualified (1 Corinthians 9:27).

It seems that Paul has contradicted himself. In the first set of verses, he confidently claims that nothing can disqualify him. However, in the next verse, he goes on to express his concern about the possibility that he indeed might be disqualified.

Contradiction or compatibility? The latter!

We can only partially reconcile these verses, but here is my attempt:

> *Although we will not be disqualified, we have to run the race as if we could be. Indeed, if Paul stopped running the race and walked away from the Lord, the Lord would walk away from him. However, the Lord won't allow this to happen—and Paul also must not allow this to happen!*

Double-talk? To our thinking, yes. However, we should also assume, like the scientists who embrace both particle and Newtonian physics, that these sets of data are somehow compatible.

Well then, are we absolutely safe in the Lord, relying totally on His sovereignty? Yes!

Must we then expend our energies, actively pressing on for the crown of life? Again, yes!

We should take comfort in the fact that nothing can separate us from our Savior. However, this confidence we have in Him should push us forward to make our calling and election certain:

- Therefore, my brothers, be all the more eager to make your calling and election sure…(2 Peter 1:10a)

Please understand, I am not teaching against systematic theology—the attempt to understand all of Scripture in a harmonious way. Instead, I simply want to point out the dangers of pushing our theories too far, to the detriment of Scripture.

After all, there are indeed some mysteries of the faith!

Chapter 10

THE FOUNDATION OF OUR THEOLOGY

CHAPTER SUMMARY

According to Jesus and all of the biblical authors, our theology must be derived from the Bible. And yet, God also reveals and instructs us through His General Revelation, His creation. However, Scripture must remain supreme.

What are the building blocks of our theology? From where must we derive our Christian worldview, our basic beliefs?

From Scripture, of course.

Jesus had the highest possible opinion of Scripture. He regarded all of it as the very Words of God. When tempted by the Devil, He relied exclusively on Scripture:

- Jesus answered [the Devil], "It is written: 'Man does not live on bread alone, but on every word that comes from the mouth of God'" (Matthew 4:4).

Jesus never set Himself above Scripture. He never considered Himself its judge, deciding which verses were truly inspired. He received "every word" as God's Word:

- "Do not think that I have come to abolish the Law or the Prophets; I have not come to abolish them but to fulfill them. I tell you the truth, until heaven and earth disappear, not the smallest letter, not the least stroke of a pen, will by any means disappear from the Law until everything is accomplished" (Matthew 5:17-18).

If Jesus had regarded the Word as being errant in some respect, He would never have said, "…until *everything* is accomplished." Instead, He would have said, "…until *every part that is without error* is accomplished." The plain truth is that He continually insisted that everything in the Scriptures, everything that was written, had to be fulfilled:

- He said to them, "How foolish you are, and how slow of heart to believe all that the prophets have spoken! Did not the Christ have to suffer these things and then enter his glory?" And beginning with Moses and all the Prophets, he explained to them what was said in all the Scriptures concerning himself…He said to them, "This is what I told you while I was still with you: Everything must be fulfilled that is written about me in the Law of Moses, the Prophets and the Psalms." Then he opened their minds so they could understand the Scriptures (Luke 24: 25-27, 44-45).

Notice how Jesus "opened their minds so they could understand the Scriptures." The Words of God were always of paramount importance to Christ. Whenever He quoted from them, He always affirmed what Scripture said. Never once did He disparage Scripture. Instead, He castigated those who did not know the Scriptures:

- Jesus replied, "You are in error because you do not know the Scriptures or the power of God" (Matthew 22:29).

Clearly, Jesus was speaking here to those who did not know Scripture. And the reason for their ignorance was their failure to esteem and honor it as valid, despite their protestations to the contrary:

- "But do not think I will accuse you before the Father. Your accuser is Moses, on whom your hopes are set.

If you believed Moses, you would believe me, for he wrote about me. But since you do not believe what he wrote, how are you going to believe what I say?" (John 5:45-47)

In stark contrast to the religious leadership, Jesus believed in what Moses had written. He believed that Scripture could not be broken or ignored at will (John 10:35).

Jesus specifically mentioned the Psalms as ultimately authored by God. We can see this plainly when Jesus, quoting from Psalm 110, claimed that David was "speaking by the Spirit":

- He said to them, "How is it then that David, speaking by the Spirit, calls him 'Lord'?" (Matthew 22:43)

Never once did Jesus question the divine origin of a single verse. Consequently, if we are serious about Jesus, we must embrace the same view of the Scriptures as He.

Paul certainly did. He declared all Scripture as fully God-breathed:

- All Scripture is breathed out by God and profitable for teaching, for reproof, for correction, and for training in righteousness, that the man of God may be complete, equipped for every good work (2 Timothy 3:16-17).

Paul also conducted himself in accord with the teachings of his Savior. Like Jesus, he knew that he was required to live according to the entire Word of God. His preaching and teaching reflected this truth:

- "Therefore I testify to you this day that I am innocent of the blood of all, for I did not shrink from declaring to you the whole counsel of God" (Acts 20:26-27).

Paul understood that he could not discard any of the teachings of God merely because they might be unpopular in the prevailing culture. Moreover, just like the other Apostles who wrote Holy Script, Paul regarded his epistles as the very Words of God (1 Thessalonians 2:13; 2 Peter 3:2, 15-16).

* * * * *

However, God also reveals Himself in other ways.

The Word of God in the Scriptures is called His Special Revelation. But God also reveals Himself through what is called His General Revelation. This is God's revelation through His creation, through what He has made.

Scripture points out that, through His General Revelation, everyone knows about God:

- For the wrath of God is revealed from heaven against all ungodliness and unrighteousness of men, who by their unrighteousness suppress the truth. For what can be known about God is plain to them, because God has shown it to them. For his invisible attributes, namely, his eternal power and divine nature, have been clearly perceived, ever since the creation of the world, in the things that have been made. So they are without excuse (Romans 1:18-20).

Everyone knows these universal truths about God because of His General Revelation to humankind through the created world and nature.

Yet, ordinarily, we reject and suppress these truths, even to the point of trying to rid them from our awareness.

Nevertheless, because these truths about God have been clearly shown to us, we—including people of other religions—remain guilty before God.

We also have God's laws written on our hearts. Therefore, we are without excuse. We simply cannot say that we don't know any better:

- For when Gentiles, who do not have the law, by nature do what the law requires, they are a law to themselves, even though they do not have the law. They show that the work of the law is written on their hearts, while their conscience also bears witness, and their conflicting thoughts accuse or even excuse them (Romans 2:14-15).

This is precisely why, when we choose to go against the law of God written in our conscience, we experience "conflicting thoughts"—guilt and shame. After all, we know better. And that is why we feel condemned.

God reveals many things through His General Revelation, even His love for the human race. In Lystra, we see this in Paul's words to the polytheists living there:

- "Yet he did not leave himself without witness, for he did good by giving you rains from heaven and fruitful seasons, satisfying your hearts with food and gladness" (Acts 14:17).

In Athens, Paul affirmed what the Greek poets had learned from God's General Revelation:

- "'In him [God] we live and move and have our being'; as even some of your own poets have said, 'For we are indeed his offspring.' Being then God's offspring, we ought not to think that the divine being is like gold or silver or stone, an image formed by the art and imagination of man" (Acts 17:28-29).

Paul castigated the Athenians for worshiping idols. Why was he justified in doing this? He could do this because of what had been revealed to them through God's General Revelation.

As we have clearly seen, this General Revelation of God to humanity plays an essential role. Furthermore—and perhaps a surprise to some—we need His General Revelation to help us to understand the Bible, His Special Revelation.

How could we understand God's mercy and forgiveness if we had never experienced guilt and shame because of the law written on our hearts? How could we comprehend and experience the hope of eternal life if we hadn't experienced the despair that comes in this temporary, earthly life?

Without General Revelation, how could we understand a simple verse like this one?

- Let your foot be seldom in your neighbor's house, lest he have his fill of you and hate you (Proverbs 25:17).

Because of General Revelation and the truths about life that we have learned from it, we would never be so childish as to respond like this:

> *Well, instead of actually setting foot in my neighbor's house, I will just roll in on a wheelchair. My foot will never hit the floor. That way I can ensure that my neighbors won't hate me.*

Of course, this sounds ridiculous. However, without General Revelation and the wisdom that comes with it as we live our lives, we would be highly susceptible to such erroneous interpretations of Scripture.

* * * * *

Clearly, we need both Special Revelation (SR) and General Revelation (GR), but how do we combine them? Sometimes they disagree. How do we live so that both forms of revelation can coexist harmoniously in our lives?

Here is a very practical example that illustrates this dilemma...

The Bible (SR) guarantees that when we confess our sins, God will forgive and cleanse us (1 John 1:9). However, we often don't feel cleansed immediately after confessing (GR). Which source of revelation is the accurate barometer of reality in a situation like this?

While our feelings are part of God's General Revelation, they are often distorted by a number of emotional, societal and even familial factors. Consequently, we might not be feeling or seeing our circumstances accurately. In view of this, the Bible (SR) is the surer and more authoritative standard and should be given the final say.

Jesus criticized the Pharisees for placing their traditions—the corporate "wisdom" of their elders—above Scripture:

- He answered them, "And why do you break the commandment of God for the sake of your tradition? For God commanded, 'Honor your father and your mother,' and, 'Whoever reviles father or mother must surely die.' But you say, 'If anyone tells his father or his mother, "What you would have gained from me is given to God," he need not honor his father.' So for the sake of your tradition you have made void the word of God. You hypocrites! Well did Isaiah prophesy of you, when he said: "'This people honors me with their lips, but their heart is far from me; in vain do they worship

me, teaching as doctrines the commandments of
men'" (Matthew 15:3-9).

The wisdom of the elders of Judaism had the appearance of
wisdom, connected as it was with the wisdom that comes from
experience and the passing of time. These are by-products of
General Revelation.

However, that kind of wisdom should never be raised to the
level of Scripture. Often, the wisdom of the elders had
superseded Scripture, turning their worship into a vain ritual.
Instead, we need to rely on Scripture to provide the light and
guidance we need when assessing matters of General
Revelation.

In fact, Paul warned that this was the essence of our battle—to
bring all of our thoughts and philosophies into conformity with
Scripture:

- For the weapons of our warfare are not of the flesh but
  have divine power to destroy strongholds. We destroy
  arguments and every lofty opinion raised against the
  knowledge of God, and take every thought captive to
  obey Christ (2 Corinthians 10:4-5).

Spiritual warfare is a battle over the mind. It requires us to make
sure that Scripture prevails over every other thought and belief.
According to Galatians 5:9, a little yeast can ferment and
corrode our faith. Therefore, we need to be vigilant and examine
every facet of what we believe.

Should we consider the findings of science as weighty and
authoritative as the teachings of Scripture? And what happens
when these "worldviews" disagree, as they sometimes do?
Scripture, when understood properly, must prevail.

However, this is often not the case.

The Church has a sad history of pursuing the culture instead of leading the culture by enlightening it. This also pertains to scientific findings. Why was it that the Church for years believed in geo-centrism—the notion that the sun revolves around the earth? The unfortunate truth is that the Church was following the lead of the predominant science of the day!

Why did the Church adopt the "steady state" theory, claiming that the universe has always existed? Because the science of its day had adopted this theory! And even though this idea was in direct opposition to Genesis 1:1, the Church chose the ideas and fruit of General Revelation over Scripture.

This brings us to the final point. What does God want from us? How do we honor our Savior? The answer is simple... *we honor Him by believing and proclaiming His Words:*

- If anyone speaks, he should do it as one speaking the very words of God...so that in all things God may be praised through Jesus Christ...(I Peter 4:11)

- And when they say to you, "Inquire of the mediums and the necromancers who chirp and mutter," should not a people inquire of their God? Should they inquire of the dead on behalf of the living? To the teaching and to the testimony! If they will not speak according to this word, it is because they have no dawn (Isaiah 8:19-20).

So then, let us be people who do most surely have a dawn, people who speak according to His Word!

Chapter 11

THE VARIOUS APPROACHES TO THEOLOGY

CHAPTER SUMMARY
Most of the time, when we think of theology, we are thinking of systematic theology. But there are also other enriching ways to do theology, other approaches. Historical theology investigates how the Fathers of the faith understood the Bible and how their understanding affected the Church and its doctrines. Biblical theology investigates how God's revelation was progressively revealed throughout the Bible.

In this chapter, we will discuss three different approaches to theology.

SYSTEMATIC THEOLOGY

Usually, when we are trying to understand the overall meaning of the Bible, we are doing systematic theology—the attempt to line up everything in the Bible so that it all fits together harmoniously.

> *What must I do to be saved? Should I just believe or should I also repent and obey?*

When we struggle with questions like these, we are trying to reconcile all the various verses in the Bible on this subject.

Here's another example to consider. In I Corinthians 8:4-13, the Apostle Paul wrote that we have freedom to eat, even at a pagan temple. However, some verses in Revelation indicate that we do not have this freedom:

- "But I [Jesus] have a few things against you [the church at Pergamum]: you have some there who hold the teaching of Balaam, who taught Balak to put a stumbling block before the sons of Israel, so that they might eat food sacrificed to idols and practice sexual immorality" (Revelation 2:14).

- "But I [Jesus] have this against you, that you tolerate that woman Jezebel, who calls herself a prophetess and is teaching and seducing my servants to practice sexual immorality and to eat food sacrificed to idols" (Revelation 2:20).

Once again, when we attempt to resolve apparent contradictions like these, we are engaging in systematic theology.

How then do we reconcile this dilemma concerning the food we eat? The critical issue here is not the actual eating of food which has been offered to idols. What really matters is what one believes about such activity. It is apparent that the false teachers in these churches were teaching that believers should eat this food in order to receive some sort of spiritual benefit. Otherwise, they wouldn't have recommended it.

Paul knew that it was impossible for any food to have such an influence.

We find the same kind of seeming contradiction in Paul's teaching regarding circumcision. On the one hand, Paul taught against it:

- Look: I, Paul, say to you that if you accept circumcision, Christ will be of no advantage to you. I testify again to every man who accepts circumcision that he is obligated to keep the whole law. You are severed from Christ, you who would be justified by the law; you have fallen away from grace (Galatians 5:2-4).

However, it was this same Paul of Tarsus who had Timothy circumcised:

- Paul wanted Timothy to accompany him, and he took him and circumcised him because of the Jews who were in those places, for they all knew that his father was a Greek (Acts 16:3).

At first, it might look like Paul had contradicted his own teaching. However, we need to remember that Paul's concern was not the physical act of circumcision. Even though Paul had also been circumcised, his main concern was what Christians believed about it. Once we understand this, the "contradiction" disappears. It was fine for Timothy to be circumcised, as long as he knew that it was not a requirement for his salvation.

HISTORICAL THEOLOGY

Historical theology looks at how we have understood the Bible and God over the centuries, how this understanding has evolved, and how it has affected the Church and its doctrines.

It is helpful to understand how Calvin and Luther, among others, understood the Word of God. Why is this so? Because we tend to be products of our culture and even our denominations. As a consequence, some of what we understand about the Bible might be wrong. Therefore, it helps us to see how others have understood it.

For example, I find some of Augustine's reflections refreshing:

- True happiness is to rejoice in the truth, for to rejoice in the truth is to rejoice in you, O God, who are the truth...Man's love of truth is such that when he loves something which is not the truth, he pretends to himself that what he loves is the truth, and because he hates to be proved wrong, he will not allow himself to be convinced that he is deceiving himself. So he hates the real truth for the sake of what he takes to his heart in its place (Augustine XI:23).

I also appreciate the way that Augustine describes so poignantly the way that a neglect of the Word carries its own punishment—darkness:

- I am aglow with its fire. It is the light of Wisdom, Wisdom itself, which at times shines upon me, parting my clouds. But when I weakly fall away from its light, those clouds envelop me again in the dense mantle of darkness which I bear for my punishment (Augustine XI:9).

Augustine writes in a way that few do today. For one thing, he exulted in a low self-esteem, which is so contrary to the spirit of our age:

- For I am needy and poor, but you who care for us, yet are free from care for yourself, have enough and to spare for all those who call upon you (Augustine XI:2).

- By confessing our own miserable state and acknowledging your mercy towards us, we open our hearts to you, so that you may free us wholly, as you have already begun to do. Then we shall no longer be miserable in ourselves but will find true happiness in you (Augustine XI:1).

There is much to enjoy in these old writings. However, it is good for us to remember, as we explore these ancient words, that the Church Fathers were far from faultless in their theology.

Regarding the martyrdom of the saints, the late historian, Philip Schaff, wrote that two of the Fathers, Origen and Cyprian, believed that...

- "...their prayers before the throne of God were thought to be particularly efficacious" (Schaff 83).

Furthermore, a statement by Origin...

- "...ascribes to the martyrs an atoning virtue for others" (Schaff 83).

Finally, here is what Tertullian believed:

- "Martyrs entered immediately into the blessedness of heaven, and were not required, like ordinary Christians, to pass through the intermediate state" (Schaff 83).

Where did these men get such beliefs? It seems that they had misunderstood this verse:

- Now I rejoice in my sufferings for your sake, and in my flesh I am filling up what is lacking in Christ's afflictions for the sake of his body, that is, the church (Colossians 1:24).

It sounds as if Paul was saying that the Cross of Christ was inadequate—that Paul and the other martyrs would be required, of necessity, to add something to the atoning value of the Cross.

However, there is no reason to assume this.

What would Paul be "filling up" in regard to "what is lacking in Christ's afflictions"? In fact, what must *all Christians* "fill up"? According to 2 Corinthians 5:19, we are all called to be ambassadors for Christ! We must evangelistically carry forth and proclaim the atonement already purchased by our Savior. And, as we do this, we will experience the painful fires of refinement, partaking in Christ's afflictions (2 Corinthians 4:7-11).

It is only through the pain of His refining work in us that we can fulfill this calling.

BIBLICAL THEOLOGY

There is also biblical theology, whose contribution to the Church is to provide a different focus on Scripture. In biblical theology, we are presented with the chronological and gradual unfolding of God's Word.

While systematic theology regards Scripture somewhat statically, biblical theology regards it progressively—how Scripture has revealed more of its treasure over time.

Have you ever wondered how our salvation after the Cross is different from salvation before the Cross? Or…how should we apply the Old Testament law in New Testament times?

If you have ever pondered such things, you are asking questions that concern biblical theology.

To answer the questions I mentioned above, theologians have come up with different answers. Some emphasize the discontinuity between the Old Testament (OT) and the New Testament (NT). Those who take this position argue that there have been abrupt, basic changes since Christ came to earth. Therefore, OT laws no longer apply.

Others emphasize continuity between the testaments. They assert that the OT still represents the wisdom of God and that it is part of the one, continuous plan of God. The adherents of this position emphasize the fact that the NT quotes the OT hundreds of times. This is a convincing indication that the NT writers still regarded the OT as authoritative.

Furthermore, the NT consistently asserts that all of the Scriptures—of course, including the OT—are the Words of God:

- All Scripture is breathed out by God and profitable for teaching, for reproof, for correction, and for training in righteousness, that the man of God may be complete, equipped for every good work (2 Timothy 3:16-17).

This means that even though we Christians are no longer under the Mosaic Law, its teachings are still instructive and therefore, "profitable."

But if we were to dig a little deeper here, what then does this continuity say about OT laws regarding issues like tithing, keeping the Sabbath, serving in the military, and capital punishment?

When we try to apply the OT teachings on honoring the Sabbath to the NT teachings, we find that we must still uphold the Sabbath, according to Romans 3:31. That would be a point of continuity between the OT and the NT.

But if we look at another set of verses in Romans, we observe that there is also discontinuity. We discover that we are free to honor the Sabbath, but in different ways:

- One person esteems one day as better than another, while another esteems all days alike. Each one should be fully convinced in his own mind. The one who observes the day, observes it in honor of the Lord. The one who eats, eats in honor of the Lord, since he gives thanks to God, while the one who abstains, abstains in honor of the Lord and gives thanks to God (Romans 14:5-6).

It is interesting to note that perhaps this flexibility had already been built into the Mosaic Law. After all, Jesus reminded His critics that the priests worked on the Sabbath; babies were circumcised on the Sabbath; and farmers took care of their animals on the Sabbath.

Indeed, there are many things that have remained unchanged between the two Covenants. Here are just a few:

> The nature of God and man;
> our relationship to God based upon faith, confession, repentance, and obedience;
> salvation based upon the mercy of God;
> the moral prohibitions against stealing, lying, murder, adultery, and kidnapping.

However, we are no longer required to circumcise our children, make offerings at a temple, or even to fast. Many things have been fulfilled and, therefore, no longer need to be obeyed:

- Therefore let no one pass judgment on you in questions of food and drink, or with regard to a festival or a new moon or a Sabbath. These are a shadow of the things to come, but the substance belongs to Christ (Colossians 2:16-17).

As the repository of those shadows or symbols of what was to come, the OT remains both instructive and encouraging.

Encouraging? Yes!

I teach a course called *Christ in the Old Testament.* In this class, I try to show how the Messiah is progressively revealed in the OT, starting with the faintest shadow of a prophecy in Genesis 3:14-15. Here we find that the "seed of the woman" will overcome evil. Perhaps this same seed, or offspring, will become a blessing to the entire world (Genesis 12:1-3).

Later, it is revealed that a strange being, often called the "Angel of the Lord," is playing a pivotal role among the Israelites. In fact, it becomes increasingly apparent that this Angel is Yahweh (Genesis 16:13; 19:18). Jacob wrestles with this Angel and discovers that he is actually wrestling with God. Miraculously, Jacob does not die (Genesis 32).

Moses later encounters the Angel in the burning bush, discovering that this Angel is indeed God. Moses removes his sandals because he knows that he is standing on holy ground (Exodus 3:2-5).

These indicators of Christ in the OT are important, especially since the Rabbis insist that God cannot appear in human form.

The Rabbis also accuse us Christians of misusing their Hebrew Scriptures by claiming that they provide evidence for the Trinity. Although the evidence we find in the OT is not as explicit as in the NT, it is still there nonetheless: Genesis 1:2, 26-27; 3:22; 11:7; 19:24; Psalm 2:7, 12; 110:1; Isaiah 7:14; 9:6; 11; 44:6; 48:16; 63:9; Jeremiah 23:5-6; Ezekiel 2:2-3; 11:5; Hosea 1:7; Micah 5:2; Zechariah 2:10-11; 4:6; 12:10; Malachi 3:1-3.

I sometimes challenge my students to identify one NT doctrine that is not found, in some form, in the OT. They cannot do it.

Both Testaments represent the one, progressively-revealed plan of God. This is encouraging because it reveals that such continuity, even at the deepest levels, can only be explained if the Bible has one supreme Author.

Knowing this affects the way we interpret Scripture.

* * * * *

While it is important to try to understand the Bible according to the intent of the human authors and the way that the "audience" of those authors would have understood their words, we must not limit our interpretations in light of these perspectives.

We need to remember always that, because they were dealing with the Words of God Himself, there would be much that the human authors would *not* understand about what they were led to write! They had even been counselled about this:

- Concerning this salvation, the prophets who prophesied about the grace that was to be yours searched and inquired carefully, inquiring what person or time the Spirit of Christ in them was indicating when he predicted the sufferings of Christ and the subsequent glories. It was revealed to them [by the Spirit] that they were serving not themselves but you, in the things that have now been announced to you through those who preached the good news to you by the Holy Spirit sent from heaven, things into which angels long to look (1 Peter 1:10-12).

Amazingly, much of what had been written was not written for its original audience—the children of Israel. Instead, it was written *for us!*

But how can this be so? We Christians already have the full revelation of the NT. Why do we also need to study the prophets of Israel? The prophets of Israel are essential because their writings provide us with *powerful confirmation and assurance of the Gospel!*

I think there is a tendency to minimize the importance of the full revelation of God that is presented in the pages of the Gospel. Without this revelation, the Israelites stumbled in relative darkness.

We find evidence of this even in the writings of Israel's wisest man, Solomon. Because his quest for wisdom had failed to provide him with the glorious revelation of what God was preparing for His children, Solomon complained:

- Then I said in my heart, "What happens to the fool will happen to me also. Why then have I been so very wise?" And I said in my heart that this also is vanity… So I hated life, because what is done under the sun was grievous to me, for all is vanity and a striving after wind. I hated all my toil in which I toil under the sun, seeing that I must leave it to the man who will come after me, and who knows whether he will be wise or a fool? Yet he will be master of all for which I toiled and used my wisdom under the sun. This also is vanity. So I turned about and gave my heart up to despair over all the toil of my labors under the sun (Ecclesiastes 2:15-20).

Solomon wasn't toiling like others, but his life was oppressive to him. Why? From the perspective of his great wisdom, life was without meaning and, therefore, burdensome. Even through the eyes of his wisdom, he could not fathom any meaningful advantage of humanity over the beast:

- For what happens to the children of man and what happens to the beasts is the same; as one dies, so dies the other. They all have the same breath, and man has no advantage over the beasts, for all is vanity. All go to one place. All are from the dust, and to dust all return. Who knows whether the spirit of man goes upward and the spirit of the beast goes down into the earth? So I saw that there is nothing better than that a man should rejoice in his work, for that is his lot. Who can bring him to see what will be after him? (Ecclesiastes 3:19-22)

Why didn't Solomon know about heaven? Hadn't Moses written about this final reward? Not explicitly. Yes, Solomon's father

David had written about dwelling with the Lord forever, but perhaps Solomon regarded David's Psalms as more about a figurative reality rather than a concrete, physical one. Or perhaps Solomon just wasn't sure.

In any event, despite his wisdom about the things of this world, it seems that Solomon was uncertain about the next world, the very thing that he needed to know.

However, we—inheritors through Christ of the wisdom and blessings found in both covenants—are the beneficiaries of our Lord's progressive revelation, enabling us to glory in His Gospel:

- We have this as a sure and steadfast anchor of the soul, a hope that enters into the inner place behind the curtain, where Jesus has gone as a forerunner on our behalf, having become a high priest forever after the order of Melchizedek (Hebrews 6:19-20).

Works Cited

Augustine. *Confessions*. Penguin Classics, 1981.

Schaff, Philip. *History of the Christian Church*. Arkose Press, 2015.

Chapter 12

OUR CHRISTIAN BELIEFS

CHAPTER SUMMARY
It is hard to believe that our beliefs make a difference, especially when it comes to salvation. Consequently, many charge that God's requirement of faith is unfair and arbitrary. They say that salvation should depend on the condition of the heart. However, our beliefs are the fruit of hearts that have been changed. Oprah Winfrey and David Benner offer faiths without set beliefs; in other words, faiths without doctrine.

Truth matters—it has the power to transform!

- Do not conform any longer to the pattern of this world, but be transformed by the renewing of your mind (Romans 12:2a).

One skeptic charged:

> *You Christians have it all wrong. God doesn't care about your dogmatic beliefs, but the condition of your heart. What we believe is superficial and unimportant. It's the intents of our heart that matter.*

Actually, there is some truth in what the skeptic is saying. The condition of the heart is indeed all-important. This is why Jesus taught that we have to be born again (John 3:3, 5).

However, Jesus did not pull this idea out of thin air. Instead, the need for a new and God-centered heart is a Hebrew concept. Jeremiah claimed that a new—or renewed— heart is at the very foundation of God's plan for His people:

- "They will be my people, and I will be their God. I will give them singleness of heart and action, so that they will always fear me and that all will then go well for them and for their children after them. I will make an everlasting covenant with them: I will never stop doing good to them, and I will inspire them to fear me, so that they will never turn away from me" (Jeremiah 32:38-40).

Everything must start with a change of heart. Why is this? A changed heart is essential because we have all become God's enemies (Romans 5:8-10; 3:10-16). Therefore, it is our hardened heart that must be converted first:

- "I will sprinkle clean water on you, and you will be clean; I will cleanse you from all your impurities and from all your idols. I will give you a new heart and put a new spirit in you; I will remove from you your heart of stone and give you a heart of flesh. And I will put my Spirit in you and move you to follow my decrees and be careful to keep my laws" (Ezekiel 36:25-27).

The state of our heart determines how we behave and the way we think and believe. It is from our heart that we speak. When our heart is softened, we are drawn to the light of truth—the light that comes from God (John 3:19-21). As we grow in our faith, we learn to embrace the light...and the truth and the wisdom of God that flows from it.

When Jesus perceived that a teacher had answered Him with wisdom, He observed:

- "You are not far from the kingdom of God" (Mark 12:34).

Why is there such a fundamental association between wisdom and closeness to God?

Wisdom comes from a heart that has been made responsive to the things of God—to faith, righteousness, and obedience. Wisdom, therefore, reflects the work of God in us.

Jesus saw this wisdom in a centurion. The Roman soldier understood that he was not worthy that Jesus should come to his house:

- [Jesus] was amazed and said to those following him, "Truly I tell you, I have not found anyone in Israel with such great faith" (Matthew 8:10).

Wisdom, faith, humility, obedience—all of these are associated qualities, each arising from a heart prepared and nourished by God.

Of course, Jesus was able to recognize these qualities in the life of a Canaanite woman. When she stated humbly that she was willing to eat the crumbs [of truth] left by the Jews, just as a dog would, He marveled at her faith:

- Then Jesus said to her, "Woman, you have great faith! Your request is granted." And her daughter was healed at that moment (Matthew 15:28).

Her faith was a faith in Jesus. It was a living faith, associated with wisdom and humility, and arising from a heart enlivened by grace.

Here is the underlying point—that faith is not a set of inert beliefs that we generate to assure ourselves that we won't go to hell. Rather, our beliefs are an integral part of a heart and mind that have been enabled to see the truth.

In contrast to this, skeptics charge that the beliefs of Christians are superficial and, therefore, could not possibly have anything to do with our ultimate fate. However, our faith and our beliefs are outgrowths of the new heart that we have been given. They are inseparable, like the oak that cannot be separated from the acorn from which it grew.

When we have a new heart, we are drawn to the light—the truth—and we want to walk in the light, as Jesus taught us:

- "And this is the judgment: the light has come into the world, and people loved the darkness rather than the light because their works were evil. For everyone who does wicked things hates the light and does not come to the light, lest his works should be exposed. But whoever does what is true comes to the light, so that it may be clearly seen that his works have been carried out in God" (John 3:19-21, ESV).

Ordinarily, we hate the light. It exposes our evil. That is why we feel a greater comfort in the darkness, the place where our deceit and rationalizations will not be exposed. However, when God begins to draw us, we are drawn to the truth of His light. We begin to desire to walk in that light, in our beliefs as well as in our behavior.

It is a package deal. Both a renewed heart and faith are the gift of God (Ephesians 2:8-9). They are inseparable. Therefore, faith is not superficial but a necessary outgrowth of the gift of being born-again. We believe because our Lord opened our heart to the light of His truth, as He did for Lydia:

- One of those listening was a woman from the city of Thyatira named Lydia, a dealer in purple cloth. She was a worshiper of God. The Lord opened her heart to respond to Paul's message (Acts 16:14).

We have become such lovers of darkness that we have to be strenuously drawn into the light:

114

- "No one can come to me [Jesus] unless the Father who sent me draws them, and I will raise them up at the last day" (John 6:44).

We all have to be drawn—kicking and squawking—into the light.

Paul was a prime example of this.

Prior to his conversion, he had persecuted Christians—killing or forcing them to renounce Christ. He did not suddenly decide to believe in Christ. Instead, he was struck down with blindness and then miraculously healed—internally and externally (Acts 9:1-18).

One last point to consider here: What we believe is not merely the effect or by-product of the gift of God. Our beliefs are also causal. They profoundly impact our attitudes, feelings, behavior, and relationships—even our relationship to our Savior and His salvation.

Following decades of depression and then panic attacks, it was almost impossible for me to believe that God loved me, or even anyone else. It seemed to me that God was merely being entertained by the freak show happening below Him…as He consumed a bowl of popcorn.

However, I had nowhere else to go—no other hope—so I continued to pray to Him.

If anything, my feelings told me that He must surely be a sadist. What else could explain my suffering? However, one night when I was outside praying, I realized that He couldn't be a sadist. If the Gospel accounts were in any sense true, they painted a picture of a God who loved us so much that He suffered the worst death for our sins. And, according to Romans 10:12-13, that included each and every one who calls upon the name of the Lord—even me!

This truth has never left me.

* * * * *

Well then, is it possible for us to have hearts pure enough to be saved? Oprah Winfrey thinks so:

- "God is about a feeling experience, not a believing experience…A mistake we humans make is believing that there is only one way…There are many paths to what you call God…There couldn't possibly be just one way…Do you think that if you never heard the name of Jesus but lived with a loving heart…you wouldn't get to heaven?…Does God care about the heart or if you call His Son 'Jesus'?" (Winfrey)

God does care about the heart. But what if our hearts are corrupt?

The truth of the heart's corruption is the consistent testimony of the Bible. To bring this point home, Paul, in the book of Romans, quoted extensively from the Hebrew Scriptures:

- As it is written:
  "There is no one righteous, not even one;
      there is no one who understands;
      there is no one who seeks God.
  All have turned away,
      they have together become worthless;
  there is no one who does good,
      not even one."
  "Their throats are open graves;
      their tongues practice deceit."
  "The poison of vipers is on their lips."
      "Their mouths are full of cursing and bitterness."
  "Their feet are swift to shed blood;
      ruin and misery mark their ways,

and the way of peace they do not know."
"There is no fear of God before their eyes."
Romans 3:10-18

Yes, our hearts do indeed matter. But from what we have just seen, each one of our hearts is found to be lacking and, even worse, antagonistic to its Maker. What hope then do we have? Certainly there is no hope in our worthiness, but only in the mercy of God.

But alas, not everyone agrees with this assessment.

Psychologist and professed Christian, David Benner, offers a faith similar to Oprah's. He rejects the significance of the truths and doctrines of the Gospel in favor of an alternative spirituality:

- Equating faith with beliefs truncates and trivializes spirituality by reducing it to a mental process. Thoughts are, quite simply, a poor substitute for relationship. Some Christians speak much of a personal relationship with God but assume that this is based on holding right beliefs. Is it any wonder that this attempt to reduce Ultimate Mystery to theological propositions so often results in the principle personal relationship being between a person and his or her own thoughts? Cherishing thoughts about God replaces cherishing God; knowing about the Divine replaces knowing the Divine. Whenever the Wholly Other is thought to be contained in one's beliefs and opinions, divine transcendence is seriously compromised and personal relationship with the Spirit minimized (Benner 6).

Not only does Benner disparage the notion that God saves through what we believe, but he disparages belief and its doctrines entirely!

He claims that "Cherishing thoughts about God replaces cherishing God." However, this is miles away from the teachings of Jesus who, without any reservations, equated truth and knowledge with true worship:

- "But the hour is coming, and is now here, when the true worshipers will worship the Father in spirit and truth, for the Father is seeking such people to worship him. God is spirit, and those who worship him must worship in spirit and truth" (John 4:23-24, ESV).

Jesus never suggested that God can be served or worshiped apart from the truth of His Word. Instead, if we love and cherish Him, we need to do so in accordance with His teachings:

- Jesus answered him, "If anyone loves me, he will keep my word, and my Father will love him, and we will come to him and make our home with him. Whoever does not love me does not keep my words. And the word that you hear is not mine but the Father's who sent me" (John 14:23-24, ESV).

How did Jesus love and cherish His Father? Once again, by abiding in His Word:

- "If you keep my commandments, you will abide in my love, just as I have kept my Father's commandments and abide in his love" (John 15:10, ESV).

On a human level, when we think about the way that we cherish and treasure one another, we realize that this cherishing is deeply connected to what we understand about the other person in the relationship.

For example, I cherish my wife because of what I know about her—namely, her honesty, faithfulness, and love for me. I cannot love and cherish her apart from what I understand about her.

The same is also true about our love for God. Our love must be based on our understanding of Him and on our obedience to what we understand in His Word.

Now, let's return to Oprah…

What would be the result of a salvation based upon the goodness of our hearts? We know that Scripture has made it clear that all of our hearts are corrupt. But what if God graded on a curve, granting salvation to those who have the best and most loving hearts?

This would cause an even greater problem in our relationship with God. If we "passed the test," it would make us arrogant. It would make us think that we were more deserving than others. Paul warned about this very real danger:

- For consider your calling, brothers: not many of you were wise according to worldly standards, not many were powerful, not many were of noble birth. But God chose what is foolish in the world to shame the wise; God chose what is weak in the world to shame the strong; God chose what is low and despised in the world, even things that are not, to bring to nothing things that are, so that no human being might boast in the presence of God (1 Corinthians 1:26-29, ESV).

* * * * *

If I were to play devil's advocate for a moment, I would ask this question: Is arrogance and the entitlement-mentality that comes along with it really such a great problem?

When I had a higher self-esteem, I was more dissatisfied with others, including my wife. However, as God humbled me and helped me to see myself more accurately, I began to appreciate others more.

I also began to understand that salvation and everything else we receive from God can only be received as a gift, by His grace (Ephesians 2:8-9; Romans 3:26-28; Galatians 3:1-5; 5:2-4). If God were to act justly, He would destroy us all by virtue of our pitiful merits:

- For the wages of sin is death, but the gift of God is eternal life in Christ Jesus our Lord (Romans 6:23).

That is why our only hope is in the mercy of God!

Ultimately, we are saved by a renewed heart with renewed desires and intentions:

- "I will sprinkle clean water on you, and you will be clean; I will cleanse you from all your impurities and from all your idols. I will give you a new heart and put a new spirit in you; I will remove from you your heart of stone and give you a heart of flesh. And I will put my Spirit in you and move you to follow my decrees and be careful to keep my laws. You will live in the land I gave your forefathers; you will be my people, and I will be your God" (Ezekiel 36:25-28).

- But when the kindness and love of God our Savior appeared, he saved us, not because of righteous things we had done, but because of his mercy. He saved us through the washing of rebirth and renewal by the Holy Spirit, whom he poured out on us generously through Jesus Christ our Savior, so that, having been justified by his grace, we might become heirs having the hope of eternal life (Titus 3:4-7).

Once we have a renewed heart, we also have renewed beliefs and intentions, as part of the New Covenant promise.

Therefore, faith is not something artificial and sterile. It is having our eyes opened to see and receive the truth which was always apparent but always previously rejected. Faith is something that arises and is received as our heart is changed:

- "I will give them singleness of heart and action, so that they will always fear me for their own good and the good of their children after them. I will make an everlasting covenant with them: I will never stop doing good to them, and *I will inspire them to fear me*, so that they will never turn away from me" (Jeremiah 32:39-40, emphasis added).

- "But the one who received the seed that fell on good soil [having a renewed heart] is the man *who hears the word and understands it*. He produces a crop, yielding a hundred, sixty or thirty times what was sown" (Matthew 13:23, emphasis added).

In light of all this, it is certainly not our thoughts alone that save us. The Devil also has the right thoughts in this regard. According to James 2:19, he knows the truth. Instead, it is the gift of a renewed heart which opens our eyes to the truths and doctrines of the Gospel and inclines us to receive them.

* * * * *

Meanwhile, returning to Benner—his viewpoint is incoherent and illogical. He argues for a faith that only contains a trust in God without an understanding of the One we are to trust!

Well then, what differentiates our Savior from the god of Islam or the god of the New Age? Doctrines!

We can trust in Christ because we believe what He tells us—that we are no longer guilty of sin and that we will be with Him for eternity. Without such doctrines, trust has no foundation or even meaning. It is without form and cannot be embraced. And even if we did embrace such a faith, we would be trusting in a vague, subjective feeling—a faith without content.

What—specifically—would I be able to trust about such a god?

I would have to trust in my feelings about Him. And yet, in my case, it was my feelings that plagued me with self-contempt. By my feelings I was convinced that God hated me. It was only the Spirit working through Scripture that convinced me otherwise. He assured me that my feelings did not reflect His truth, but were only a reflection of my mixed-up, messed-up past.

However, this leaves the Christian faith vulnerable to another challenge:

> *If faith/salvation is a gift from God, and no one can earn or deserve it, it is unfair to condemn those who have not received this gift!*

While we cannot earn or deserve salvation, we can certainly cry out to God to forgive our sins and to receive us. After all, we know that we are sinners. We experience guilt and shame. But instead of dealing honestly with our spiritual brokenness and failure, we deny and rationalize and justify our sins, as Jesus revealed:

- "This is the verdict: Light has come into the world, but men loved darkness instead of light because their deeds were evil. Everyone who does evil hates the light, and will not come into the light for fear that his deeds will be exposed" (John 3:19-20).

In stark contrast with those who choose to remain in the dark, Jesus gave us a portrait of someone coming into the light. He told a parable about two people praying in the Temple. One trusted in his own righteousness and prayed accordingly. The other, a hated tax-collector, confessed that he was a rank sinner who could not even begin to trust in his non-existent personal merit. He realized that his only hope was in the undeserved mercy of God.

Jesus explained:

- "I tell you, this man went down to his house justified, rather than the other. For everyone who exalts himself will be humbled, but the one who humbles himself will be exalted" (Luke 18:14).

Humility is a matter of facing the truth about our merit-less and hopeless situation.

Sadly, this was not the condition or state of mind of Israel, as God revealed through the Prophet Jeremiah:

- "Does a maiden forget her jewelry, a bride her wedding ornaments? Yet my people [Israel] have forgotten me, days without number...On your clothes men find the lifeblood of the innocent poor, though you did not catch them breaking in. Yet in spite of all this you say, 'I am innocent; he is not angry with me.' But I will pass judgment on you because you say, 'I have not sinned'" (Jeremiah 2:32-35).

Israel had been consistently unfaithful to their God. When they sinned, they would not confess but would deny. When we in the present day also make charges that God is unfair, instead of honestly confessing our sins, we prove that we too are exactly like stiff-necked Israel.

Returning once again to David Benner, he claims that...

- Cherishing thoughts about God replaces cherishing God (Benner 6).

But is it possible to cherish God without thoughts or an understanding of God? I don't see how. To cherish God without understanding Him is to cherish *our own feelings and thoughts about God.* But this is not cherishing God. Instead, this kind of relationship with God would be merely a matter of cherishing our own imaginations about Him.

Once again, using the relationship I have with my wife as an example—I must love her for who she is in truth and not what I would like her to be.

To worship God according to our own imaginations is strictly forbidden by Scripture:

- Thus says the LORD of hosts: "Do not listen to the words of the prophets who prophesy to you, filling you with vain hopes. They speak visions of their own minds, not from the mouth of the LORD. They say continually to those who despise the word of the LORD, 'It shall be well with you'; and to everyone who stubbornly follows his own heart [that walketh after the imagination of his own heart, KJV], they say, 'No disaster shall come upon you'" (Jeremiah 23:16-17; Genesis 6:5; Proverbs 19:11; Luke 1:51).

In contrast to Benner's idea of a faith without truth or doctrine, Jesus taught that doctrine is essential:

- So Jesus said to the Jews who had believed him, "If you abide in my word, you are truly my disciples, and you will know the truth, and the truth will set you free" (John 8:31-32, ESV).

124

No truth, no freedom!

Works Cited

Benner, David G. *Soulful Spirituality: Becoming Fully Alive and Deeply Human.* BrazosPress, 2011.

Winfrey, Oprah. Uploaded 13 April 2008, www.youtube.com/watch?v=ETel6i5oqh4. Accessed 21 September 2016.

Conclusion

THEOLOGY ON OUR KNEES

CHAPTER SUMMARY
Wisdom and the understanding of Scripture is not merely a matter of mental activity. We can receive wisdom, understanding and more, from God...through prayer.

I do not want to leave you with the conclusion that theology, the Bible, and rightly dividing the Word of truth is simply a matter of study and head knowledge. In fact, I think these things are secondary.

Most importantly, theology must be conducted on our knees.

Why do I believe this? I believe it because understanding God's Word cannot be done without God and a humble and sustained relationship with Him. It is He who illuminates our minds and hearts to understand the Word—the very thing that Jesus had done for His disciples:

- Then he opened their minds to understand the Scriptures, and said to them, "Thus it is written, that the Christ should suffer and on the third day rise from the dead, and that repentance and forgiveness of sins should be proclaimed in his name to all nations, beginning from Jerusalem. You are witnesses of these things" (Luke 24:45-49).

If the minds of the disciples had to be opened by our Lord, then so too must ours! To believe otherwise is pure hubris.

Here is what Christ had to say about this:

- "For everyone who exalts himself will be humbled, and he who humbles himself will be exalted" (Luke 14:11; 18:14).

To receive from God is to be humbled before God. We need to remember this always, recognizing our utter dependency upon Him, even for our understanding.

I am therefore reminded of God's words to Job's friends:

- After the LORD had spoken these words to Job, the LORD said to Eliphaz the Temanite: "My anger burns against you and against your two friends, for you have not spoken of me what is right, as my servant Job has" (Job 42:7).

Job's three friends had spoken arrogantly about things they did not understand, and this incurred the anger of God.

God has shown me that whenever I become prideful about what I know—and this is a constant temptation—I will be humbled. Sometimes, it is simply a matter of reaping the foolishness I have sown.

Consequently, I try to commit all of my teaching, writing, and even thinking to the Lord in prayer. I have a great responsibility to those I influence and great accountability before the Lord. I must conduct myself faithfully as His servant.

Besides this, I often have a sense that what I am writing is better than what I am capable of writing. I therefore suspect that He is opening my mind to understand the Scriptures, and I want to give Him full credit for this, always.

* * * * *

THE FEAR OF THE LORD AND THEOLOGY

Our presuppositions are our most basic beliefs. They serve as a lens that colors everything else we see and believe. Of course, they also color our interpretation of Scripture. Our presuppositions are so deeply ingrained in us that they can be exposed and replaced only through prayer.

For example, I came to the Lord 40 years ago as a washed-up, radical leftist. I hated cops. I smoked pot and knew that if the police caught me, I would have to suffer the consequences. Therefore, they represented a threat to me.

When I, as a fledgling Christian, encountered the passage that instructed me to submit to all authorities—since they are from God (Romans 13:1-4)—everything within me rose up in revolt. I was sure that there had to be another interpretation of this passage besides the obvious one. Fortunately for me, there weren't any other ex-hippies around to offer any appealing alternatives. Instead, I gradually had to bite the bullet and admit the truth that was revealed in the Word.

This believing of things I did not want to believe has been my constant companion for each of the 40 years of my life in the Lord.

My deeply engraved presuppositions were so powerful that they distorted the way I read Scripture. I would underline only those verses that made me feel good about myself. And conversely, I would overlook those verses that made me feel bad. Scripture had become a martini by which I could anesthetize my spiritual senses.

Although I didn't realize it at the time, I needed the Holy Spirit to expose my biased approach.

Not surprisingly, I just could not get my mind around the idea of grace. After all, one of my presuppositions had informed me that there were no free lunches, spiritual or otherwise. I felt that I had to "earn" God's grace.

However, this presupposition contained the seeds of its own destruction. Over the years, the Spirit made it apparent to me that I could not even earn a smile from God, let alone salvation. As a result, I felt so self-condemned that I was sure that God was also condemning me.

If I was going to survive the turmoil I felt within, I knew I had to find something else in God's promises to relieve my pain, something I had been too blind to see because of my presuppositions.

I was utterly broken, but my Savior opened my eyes to a mercy which I had seen before:

- For by grace you have been saved through faith. And this is not your own doing; it is the gift of God, not a result of works, so that no one may boast (Ephesians 2:8-9).

Through suffering, the Lord removed my errant presupposition, my old dysfunctional lens. Then, and only then, was I enabled to see through a new lens—a new presupposition—that God truly loved me.

This illustrates something very important about doing theology and understanding Scripture. Once again, understanding is so much more than mental activity. Primarily, it is a matter of the Holy Spirit emptying us in order to fill us. He prunes us back so that we might be more fruitful:

- "I am the true vine, and my Father is the vinedresser. Every branch in me that does not bear fruit he takes away, and every branch that does bear fruit he prunes, that it may bear more fruit" (John 15:1-2).

We need to always remember that it is the Father Who does the pruning. We cannot do that job. And the Father does the work of purifying, as well (1 Peter 1:7; 4:12).

When He returns and opens the eyes of Israel, our Savior will also do the work of refining:

- "Behold, I send my messenger, and he will prepare the way before me. And the Lord whom you seek will suddenly come to his temple; and the messenger of the covenant in whom you delight, behold, he is coming," says the LORD of hosts. "But who can endure the day of his coming, and who can stand when he appears? For he is like a refiner's fire and like fullers' soap. He will sit as a refiner and purifier of silver, and he will purify the sons of Levi and refine them like gold and silver, and they will bring offerings in righteousness to the LORD" (Malachi 3:1-3).

Once again, this is work that we cannot do. We must pray for Him to do it.

Paul knew well the full extent of the Spirit's work. He therefore gave God all the credit, even for his own diligent labors:

- But by the grace of God I am what I am, and his grace toward me was not in vain. On the contrary, I worked harder than any of them, though it was not I, but the grace of God that is with me (1 Corinthians 15:10).

The fruit that comes forth from our lives is actually the fruit of the Spirit. That is why He must get all of the credit, even for our theological understanding.

And just what is this work of pruning and refining and purifying that He does in us? He exposes our blindness, our presuppositions and attitudes—all the fruit of our darkness.

After all, just as Jesus taught, we are lovers of the darkness. Let's look again at this passage we have examined several times before:

- "And this is the judgment: the light has come into the world, and people loved the darkness rather than the light because their works were evil. For everyone who does wicked things hates the light and does not come to the light, lest his works should be exposed" (John 3:19-20, ESV).

Ordinarily, we are such lovers of the darkness that we have convinced ourselves that we are in the light. There are so many proof-texts for this that I hope that citing just one verse will be sufficient:

- All the ways of a man are pure in his own eyes, but the LORD weighs the spirit (Proverbs 16:2).

It is painful to see that we are wrong and in error. We convince ourselves that any fault lies outside ourselves.

I was so blind that, even after coming to Christ, I had assured myself that He had chosen me because I was more worthy than others. This addictive, self-glorifying presupposition had to be burned and refined out of me. Only then was I enabled to adore God for His mercy towards this entirely unworthy vessel.

He has to humble us before He can exalt us.

I know that there are areas of blindness that remain in me. I am always discovering logs in my eyes, which obscure my sight (Matthew 7:1-5). Consequently, I am ever-dependent upon my

Savior. I rely on Him to reveal my faulty presuppositions—the basic foundational beliefs that color everything I see and believe. And this is an ongoing process.

If we are to understand Scripture, our eyes must first be cleansed, but this is painful. Wisdom requires us to acknowledge that we are unworthy servants (Luke 17:10). Until we see the truth about ourselves, we are not going to see the truth about anything that really matters. Unless we allow the Lord to purify and refine us, we will see the world through a pair of filthy lenses.

Proverbs shows us that we reject wisdom because wisdom rebukes our pride:

- "How long, O simple ones, will you love being simple? How long will scoffers delight in their scoffing and fools hate knowledge? If you turn at my reproof, behold, I will pour out my spirit to you; I will make my words known to you. Because I have called and you refused to listen, have stretched out my hand and no one has heeded, because you have ignored all my counsel and would have none of my reproof…Then they will call upon me, but I will not answer; they will seek me diligently but will not find me. Because they hated knowledge and did not choose the fear of the LORD, would have none of my counsel and despised all my reproof, therefore they shall eat the fruit of their way, and have their fill of their own devices" (Proverbs 1:22-31).

Acquiring wisdom and the understanding of Scripture, therefore, is not primarily a matter of mental activity or even of graduating from a good seminary. Instead, it begins with the "fear of the Lord"—a fear that comes to us on our knees.

May the Lord be first in our thinking…and even in our desiring!

www.ingramcontent.com/pod-product-compliance
Lightning Source LLC
Chambersburg PA
CBHW061830040426

42447CB00012B/2903